CLASS 47/s

Gavin Morrison

Ian Allan
PUBLISHING

Contents

First published 1999

ISBN 0 7110 2677 7

Published by Ian Allan Publishing an imprint of Ian Allan Publishing Ltd, Terminal House, Shepperton, Surrey TW17 8AS.
Printed by Ian Allan Printing Ltd, Riverdene Business Park, Hersham, Surrey KT12 4RG.

Code: 9910/C2

Picture Credits
All photographs are from the author's collection, except where stated.

Front cover: *No 47550* University of Durham *is looking immaculate after its recent overhaul as it stands on Eastfield depot, Glasgow on 14 July 1989. It was new to Old Oak Common as D1731 in June 1964, receiving its TOPS number of 47350 in February 1975, it was allocated No 47139, but never carried it. It received its name at Dundee station on 1 May 1982, the ceremony being performed by Lord MacKie, Vice Chancellor of the University. Note the position of the jumper cable to allow ease of coupling away from the snowplough. It was stored unserviceable on the 18 June 1996.*

Back cover: *This colourful line up was taken at Holbeck (Leeds) depot on 3 September 1990. Locos left to right are No 47522* Doncaster Enterprise *in parcels livery, full details of its history appear on page 44. Next is No 47592 in large logo blue livery. It entered traffic as D7166 at Tinsley in September 1964. Became No 47191 in March 1974, and then No 47592 in August 1983. It was named* County of Avon *in September 1983. No 47079, originally* George Jackson Churchward *is on the right in Railfreight Construction livery. Details of the locomotive appear on page 42.*

Title page: *One of the most recent colour schemes to be applied to the class is the green livery of Great Western Trains; there are currently eight Class 47s in this pool. Until June 1999 these were diagrammed mainly for Paddington-Penzance sleepers, and were only occasionally seen in daylight. They have since appeared on certain Paddington-Plymouth/ Penzance daytime workings; No 47811 is shown at Langston Rock heading the 08.22 Penzance-Paddington on 19 June 1999.*
The locomotive entered service as No D1719 in February 1964, being renumbered 47128 in April 1974, 47656 in September 1986, and acquiring its present identity in August 1989. BR blue livery replaced the original two-tone green in April 1969, and was followed by large-logo blue in September 1986, and InterCity 'Swallow' livery in January 1991. Great Western Trains

Depot allocations have been:

2.64	Cardiff Canton (new)
7.65	Bristol, Bath Road
7.66	LM Western Lines
6.68	Bescot
5.73	Bristol, Bath Road
11.74	Cardiff Canton
2.77	Laira
3.78	Cardiff Canton
10.82	Landore
1.83	Bristol, Bath Road
6.86	Gateshead
5.87	Eastfield
5.88	Bristol, Bath Road
7.95	Bristol, St Philip's Marsh
	Landore

Preface

By the time this book appears in bookshops, it will be 37 years since the first Class 47, No D1500, emerged from Brush at Loughborough. I think it is fair to assume that a large proportion of the enthusiasts who buy a copy will never have known the railways in this country without Class 47s. There are possibly still a few years to go before they completely disappear from Railtrack, but a very large number of them have been withdrawn, and they are not now to be seen all over the network on every type of working.

Allan Baker has made it clear elsewhere in the book that whilst externally members of the class appeared to be similar, internally

Above: In the days before the Aire Valley electrification the Sunday 14.30 Bradford Forster Square-King's Cross, a Class 91 working with Mk 4 coaches, was powered by a Class 47/4 between Bradford and Leeds. Parcels Sector-liveried No 47634 was on this duty on a fine 28 April 1991, with Class 91 No 91009 in tow. The following month No 47634 received the name Holbeck, No 47425 having relinquished this name in February 1991. A Western Region locomotive when new in August 1964 as No D1751, it received TOPS No 47158 in February 1974, and then 47634 in December 1985.

It has received the following liveries:
BR green, from new
BR blue with silver roof, by August 1978
BR (standard) blue, from April 1981
BR blue with silver roof, from May 1981

Large-logo blue, from December 1985
(with black window frames from July 1987 to May 1988)
Parcels Sector red/grey, from April 1991.

Allocations have been as follows:

8.64	Landore (new)
3.65	Bristol, Bath Road
3.65	Cardiff Canton
5.66	Old Oak Common
10.66	Cardiff Canton
12.67	LM Western Lines
6.68	Crewe
3.69	Bescot
10.69	Crewe
12.71	Bescot
10.72	Stratford
10.77	Immingham
5.78	Stratford
10.87	Bristol, Bath Road
2.91	Crewe.

this was far from being the case. The internal variations were in fact about as numerous as the livery variations that have appeared in the last 10 years.

I have always liked the Class 47s, although many enthusiasts paid scant attention to them over the years, no doubt because they were so common on virtually any type of train or line. It was a similar case when there were 842 Stanier Class 5s at work — everybody assumed they would always be around, and it came as quite a shock when they finally vanished. Who knows, in 30 to 40 years' time, enthusiasts may be mourning the passing of the Class 66s.

The early months of 1999 have not been the best time to try and complete this book, due to the large number of withdrawals, which have made it very difficult to make sure the captions are accurate. No doubt some of the locomotives which were in traffic at the time of writing will have been withdrawn by the time the book is published, so the word 'currently' has had to be included far more often than I would have liked.

I should particularly like to thank Peter Jaques, Richard Levett and Nigel Antolic, all members of the '47401 Project', for providing much of the detail about individual locomotives and keeping me up-to-date, which has made my task so much easier; thanks also to Nick Pigott, and to my good friend Allan Baker for his chapters on the class — it is so good to have somebody with first-hand experience of the locomotives to write about them.

Fortunately there are already several locomotives in preservation, and no doubt more to follow, but for me it will be very sad to see the day when the last Class 47-hauled train runs on Railtrack.

The day is approaching when the Class 47s will be no more, except in preservation.

Preservation Support

If you are interested in helping to preserve two of these fine locomotives, Nos 47401 and D1516, you may wish to support the 47401 Project, which can be contacted at:

21 The Oaklands
Droitwich Spa
Worcestershire WR9 8AD

Much of the detailed information about individual locomotives in this book has been supplied from the Project's database. The 47401 Project is producing a part-work named *Class 47 Data Files,* which when complete will produce a detailed history of every locomotive in the class.

Where to see preserved Class 47s (locations current May 1999):

47401 & D1516	Midland Railway Centre
D1501	East Lancashire Railway
47449	Llangollen Railway
47105	Gloucestershire & Warwickshire Railway
D1842	The Railway Age, Crewe
47643	Bo'ness & Kinneil Railway
D1705	Great Central Railway.

Introduction

With no fewer than 512 examples built, the Class 47, or Brush/Sulzer Type 4, as it was originally known, was the largest single BR main line locomotive class, and by a wide margin. There were also many more variations within this number than any other class, and this resulted in many railwaymen referring to them as the 57 varieties! The years since 1968, when the last member of the class was delivered, have seen this variety increase as locomotives have been modified, and even in the last few years, with extensive withdrawals already underway, yet another variety has emerged. This resulted from a business need for larger fuel tanks, known as long-range fuel tanks, to enable some of the locomotives to undertake longer diagrams with less opportunity to take fuel. In an effort to identify these more easily, they have been numbered in a sequence of their own in the 478xx series.

Erected both at the Brush works in Loughborough and at BR's own workshops at Crewe, in all cases with Brush electrical equipment and Sulzer engines, the first major change in design came after a mere 20 locomotives had been delivered from Loughborough. This was the result of what was, in many people's eyes (and indeed turned out to be), a retrograde step. These 20 locomotives had equipment to supply Electric Train Heating (ETH), but a decision in 1962 to retain steam heating for locomotive-hauled coaching stock on non-electrified sections of the system resulted in its omission from the production batches.

An early change thereafter was the alteration (from series-parallel to all-parallel connection) of the traction motors across the main generator, and subsequently smaller variations were many and wide-ranging. For example, no fewer than three types of steam heating equipment were fitted (and some locomotives had none at all), and there were variations in brake equipment, cooling systems, slow-speed control equipment (two different systems), load regulation and field divert control systems, the latter two as a result of the introduction of 'real' first-generation electronic equipment to traction applications. This is to name but a few! Later still, many locomotives were fitted with ETH equipment, after the earlier decision was reversed; this was different from the equipment supplied on the first 20, and indeed varied according to the connection of the traction motors. In later conversions this ETH equipment was altered again, to take advantage of developments in electronic technology.

A fundamental variation during the building programme arose from the decision to fit five locomotives with a different power unit, a Sulzer 'V' form engine being used, rather than the twin bank type used as standard. Despite some success with this unit, it was later replaced by a standard one. Much later one member of the class became a test-bed for the Class 56 engine and generator unit, being renumbered 47601 in the process; later still, as 47901, it was used for further tests, with the power unit eventually used in the Class 58 design.

When the BR locomotive fleet was renumbered, opportunity was taken to subdivide the locomotives, so as to identify to the operator the major variations of significance to how he used them. Thus, '47/0' described the 'standard' locomotives with steam heating boilers, '47/3' those without any form of train heating, and '47/4' those which were ETH-fitted — some with steam heating

boilers as well. Later, '47/7' was introduced for the Scottish Region's push-pull equipped locomotives. As we have already seen, the 478xx variant has emerged in more recent times to distinguish '47/4s' fitted with long-range fuel tanks.

During their years of service these locomotives have ventured just about everywhere on the system, and few routes have been barred to them; indeed one actually left the rails, serving as an 'exciter' at a power station for a short period! Initially allocated to the Eastern Region for use on the East Coast main line, they later found their way on to the principal passenger routes of all the Regions, including the West Coast main line north of Crewe and the Western Region (despite its preference for diesel-hydraulics); even

Above: Tinsley depot gave No 47287 the full beauty treatment for hauling the first train out of the new Europort depot near Normanton. It is shown hauling a long train (which does not appear to have been the norm since) past the site of the former Lancashire & Yorkshire steam shed at Wakefield Belle Vue, on a dismal 8 January 1996.

A Gateshead loco when new as No D1989 in February 1966, it was later allocated as follows:

9.66	York
3.67	Gateshead
10.72	Thornaby
1.85	Tinsley
9.85	Stratford
5.87	Tinsley
12.97	Crewe.

Liveries were:
BR green, when new
BR blue, by June 1974
Railfreight Distribution (original livery), from March 1989
Railfreight Distribution (revised livery), from November 1995.

Waterloo-Exeter on the Southern fell to them for a period. As well as passenger services, some members of the class went straight onto freight traffic, and the first dual-braked examples pioneered the Freightliner service — indeed they are still the mainstay of many such trains as I write these words. Despite a number of early problems, some very expensive both in terms of modifications and loss of availability, generally the class settled down well and gave consistent levels of availability and reliability,

albeit never matching the predictions made for them in the early years.

When the use of ETH started to become more widespread, as new coaching stock was introduced and older stock converted, the increasing number of ETH-equipped locomotives were used chiefly on express passenger trains. The result, a predictable decrease in their availability and reliability, was to the benefit of the remainder of the class! Unsurprisingly, the much heavier utilisation of

Above: *This is an official photograph taken by Brush Electrical Engineering Co Ltd of No D1682 when brand new outside the works at Loughborough, probably in October 1963. It was the first locomotive in the second batch to be constructed at Loughborough, and was sent new to Old Oak Common, the first Brush Type 4 for the Western Region.*

Under TOPS, No D1682 became No 47096 in May 1974; it had gained BR blue livery in 1970, and retained this until its withdrawal in July 1991 at Tinsley, where it languished until removed for scrapping at Booth's, Rotherham. It received the unofficial name of 'Rook' on 13 November 1989, which it retained to the end.

Allocations were:

10.63	Old Oak Common (new)
5.64	Saltley (WR)
4.66	LMR Western Lines
6.68	Bescot
8.72	Bristol, Bath Road
6.74	Cardiff Canton
5.85	Immingham
9.85	Tinsley
1.86	Stratford
5.89	Tinsley
7.90	stored
8.90	Tinsley
7.91	stored
7.91	withdrawn
5.94	reinstated to store
9.95	withdrawn.

the ETH locomotives, combined with the higher mileage of their diagrams and the faster speeds achieved, had adverse effects, but this was balanced by corresponding reductions in the utilisation and mileage achieved by the others. Large inroads have been made into the class recently, and their final demise is now in sight, but they are still diagrammed to attain high levels of availability and reliability, given their age. That they can still be seen on a variety of duties all over the country is evidence of that. Indeed, they remain the country's principal passenger diesel locomotive class, despite HSTs and electrification having ousted them from most InterCity services.

Although they should, and indeed with a couple more years' development could, have been a second-generation diesel design, with all the benefits that this would have brought, as events turned out they were at best of 'one and a half'-generation design technology. Nevertheless, through an obsession to phase out steam traction at all costs and as soon as possible in the misguided belief that thereby most of BR's problems would disappear, the class was produced in large numbers. For this, if for no other reason, the class deserves to be remembered in the annals of British locomotive development.

1

Parentage of the Class 47s

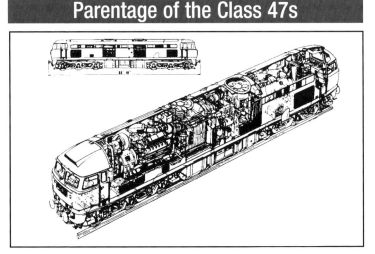

Our story starts with an Irish entrepreneur, Alan Paul Good, who came to this country from his native Dublin in 1935, with (he would later claim) but £500 in his pocket. This man was to build up a formidable portfolio of companies under his umbrella, beginning with the light oil engine manufacturers Petters of Yeovil. In the postwar boom of manufacturing industry, Good realised the potential for diesel locomotives, principally with electric transmissions, as the world's railways got back on their feet following the cessation of hostilities. After the war most railways were ordering steam locomotives in large numbers, and the manufacturers were struggling both to fulfil this demand, and to complete orders that had been placed earlier, but which had been delayed as the builders were involved in other work to assist the war effort. Good started to acquire interests in diesel engine manufacturers, beginning with the near bankrupt Petters, allegedly acquiring it for a 'song'. Later he gained control of larger firms like J. & H. McLaren, Mirrlees, Bickerton & Day, and the National Gas & Oil Engine Co. By 1946, he was on the board of no fewer than 28 undertakings, being Chairman of 22 of them, and he grouped the diesel engine manufacturers together under a holding company, Associated British Oil Engines Ltd, to which he later added Henry Meadows, amongst others. He also acquired interests in Heenan & Froude Ltd, the well-known Worcester-based hydraulic engineers, Brush Electrical Engineering Co Ltd, and Associated Locomotive Equipment Ltd, eventually becoming Chairman of all three.

Good's plans were almost complete, as he had gained control of some of the country's biggest diesel engine manufacturers, and outside the English Electric interests, among the few with any railway traction experience. However, despite having the undoubted electrical expertise of Brush, which additionally had a history of locomotive building he was in need of an established locomotive builder with mechanical parts experience, manufacturing capacity and a 'name'. When the old-established Stafford locomotive builders and general railway engineers W. G. Bagnall Ltd came on to the market in 1947, he seized his opportunity, but as at that time Brush lacked the necessary funds, he used Heenan & Froude to make the actual purchase; nevertheless, it was made clear that in the new regime, W. G. Bagnall was to take its direction from Brush.

A range of diesel-electric shunting locomotives was soon developed, and some sizeable orders obtained, principally with the Steel Company of Wales Ltd, but it was only a matter of time before something bigger came the company's way. The Crown Agents for the Colonies had invited tenders for the supply of 25 5ft 6in gauge diesel-electrics for the Ceylon Government Railway, and the contract was awarded to Brush on 13 March 1950, the largest single order yet placed in this country for main line diesel locomotives.

In February 1951, Good formed Brush-Bagnall Traction Ltd, a joint effort with people from Brush, W. G. Bagnall Ltd, and of course Heenan & Froude on its Board, to co-ordinate the combined activities and involve an established name in locomotive engineering. It was under this name therefore that the 25 locomotives were built.

The locomotives were erected at the Brush works at Loughborough, the mechanical parts (including complete bogies and underframes) being built at W. G. Bagnall's Castle Engine Works in Stafford, and the Mirrlees 12-cylinder 'V' form turbo-charged four-stroke engine coming from that company's works in

Above: In the days when the Liverpool-Newcastle services travelled via Harrogate, No D1979 nears the end of the climb from Leeds to Bramhope Tunnel with the 10.00 from Liverpool, on 10 February 1967. It was one of 13 allocated to Gateshead when new from Crewe Works in December 1965 and January 1966. Under TOPS it became No 47277 and was employed on merry-go-round traffic in West Yorkshire for several years. This locomotive was reallocated frequently in later life; after its initial spell at Gateshead.

Its allocations were as follows:

2.68	Knottingley
8.79	Healey Mills
9.84	Tinsley
9.85	Stratford
5.87	Thornaby
10.87	Immingham; then nine moves between Immingham and Cardiff Canton until:
3.93	Tinsley
1.94	Immingham
10.94	stored.

It carried the following liveries:
BR green when new
BR blue, from November 1973
BR blue with silver roof (added while at Stratford), from 16 May 1987
Railfreight Petroleum livery, from October 1989
Railfreight Distribution, from 3 April 1993.

Stalybridge. This power unit, type JS12VT, was rated at 1,000hp at 850rpm (a 200hp downrating for Ceylon), and was directly coupled to a Brush 652kW dc generator, feeding four traction motors in a series-parallel configuration. The wheel arrangement was A1A-A1A, the centre axle on each bogie being unpowered, and the completed locomotives in working order turned the scales at 87 tons.

To assist his efforts, Good head-hunted a fellow Dubliner, W. A. Smyth, who had trained with the Midland & Great Western Railway of Ireland at Broadstone, before it passed to the Great Southern Railways. Smyth had later been Chief Mechanical Engineer of the Ceylon Government Railway, and as such responsible for the prewar introduction of diesel traction in that country, Ceylon having been an early (and brave) entrant to the internal-combustion locomotive market. In 1949 Good appointed Smyth Director and General Manager of Henry Meadows Ltd, but this was merely a holding move, because in July he became a Director of W. G. Bagnall Ltd, taking over as Managing Director in March the following year, and becoming a Director of Brush-Bagnall Traction Ltd from its inception.

The Ceylon locomotives were the genesis of Brush's entry into the field of main line diesel traction, both in placing the firm on the map for prospective customers and in acquiring its valuable experience. Indeed, much experience was gained in Ceylon from the first deliveries, and many modifications were carried out to improve availability and reliability, not only with the electrical and mechanical equipment, but with the Mirrlees engine too, this being its first application for such numbers for traction purposes. Although initial deliveries had been promised

within 18 months of the order being placed, it took over twice as long before they commenced. The first five locomotives left Birkenhead Docks in January 1953, and delivery was deliberately prolonged, to allow service experience with the early deliveries. Lessons thus learned allowed modifications to be incorporated in the

Above: The external condition of many diesel locomotives in the 1960s was terrible by today's standards. No doubt this was due in part to their being stabled in grimy steam sheds. Here we see No D1923 alongside steam locomotives at Bournemouth on 23 June 1967. Originally allocated to Cardiff Canton, this locomotive was moved (along with Nos D1921/2/4-6) to Eastleigh on the Southern Region in September-October 1966. No D1934

also had a spell at Eastleigh around this time. The 'Bournemouth Belle' Pullman was one of the duties allocated to these locomotives whilst on the Southern.

The locomotive became No 47256 under TOPS, and then No 47644 in March 1986. It is currently still running as No 47756 for Rail Express Systems. This was the last Class 47 to retain BR green livery, succumbing to blue in November 1978.

remaining 20, which started to arrive from May 1954, the order being completed by October 1955. The early locomotives were modified retrospectively.

In May 1955, the British Transport Commission announced a £1,200 million Modernisation Plan for its problem child British Railways, and this encompassed the purchase

Above: The seventh of the 'Generators', No D1506 was new to Finsbury Park in January 1963, where it settled down to working East Coast main line duties for over 16 years, except for a two-year break at Immingham. The number 47407 was allocated under TOPS. From 19 August 1979 it moved to Gateshead, where it was named Aycliffe on 8 November 1984. After the Class 45/1s ended their work on trans-Pennine duties, No 47407 became a regular performer on these trains in its large-

logo blue livery.

On 16 May 1988 it was transferred to Immingham, where it remained until withdrawal in August 1990. It was often employed on dragging Class 91s between Leeds and Bradford prior to electrification. It ended its days at Scunthorpe, being cut up there in November 1995. Here we see the locomotive in happier times, heading an ecs working to Neville Hill carriage sidings, Leeds, on 8 June 1967.

Photo: N. E. Preedy

of no fewer than 2,500 main line diesel locomotives to replace steam. It was envisaged that, to gain experience, 170 locomotives would be placed in service over the ensuing two years, before quantity orders were placed. There were to be three power ranges, designated A, B and C, and covering respectively 600-800hp, 1,000-1,250hp, and 2,000hp and over, orders being placed for 400 locomotives of type A, 100 of type B and 30 of type C. Several manufacturers were involved, along with the railway workshops themselves, and it was intended there should be a number of different types within each range. Clearly, Brush-Bagnall Traction Ltd was an obvious contender for at least some of these orders, offering locomotives to cover groups A and B, and was successful with a tender for 20 A1A-A1A diesel-electrics of type B, with an engine rating of 1,250hp, the order being placed in November.

The design of the locomotives was based on the Ceylon order, with the same Mirrlees JS12VT engine, but this time rated at 1,250hp at 850rpm, and driving a Brush 823kW dc generator and four traction motors. Indeed, the original artist's impression illustrated a locomotive very like those for Ceylon, but the actual design was later refined to the familiar style known so well today. Of these 20 locomotives, the mechanical parts and bogies were built at W. G. Bagnall's Stafford works, erection being undertaken at Loughborough. The first locomotive, No D5500, took to the rails in October 1957, all 20 being in traffic by December 1958. Thus came into being the popular Brush Type 2, later Class 31, of which a further 243 examples would be built, bringing the total to 263 (the last, No D5862, being delivered in October 1962). Despite the good intentions of the 1955 BR Plan, before the prototypes had even been placed in service, in late 1957 and early 1958, large orders were placed for further diesel main line locomotives.

There were a number of variations in the Brush locomotives, particularly the engines, the first production batch (after the initial 20) having an engine uprated to deliver 1,365hp, with several being further uprated to 1,600hp, and one, No D5835, running for a while with its engine rated at 1,950hp. In all, W. G. Bagnall supplied 58 sets of mechanical parts and Commonwealth bogies for these locomotives, and Beyer Peacock and Brush themselves the remainder; all were erected at Loughborough.

Alan Good died suddenly in South Africa in 1953, and afterwards many of the companies he had tried so hard to group together began to drift apart. As W. G. Bagnall Ltd had been purchased by Heenan & Froude, and not Brush, the Brush-Bagnall partnership faltered, and the company was re-formed as Brush Traction Ltd in January 1956, with the Bagnall- and Heenan & Froude-sponsored members leaving the Board. Thereafter, there was no 'official' connection between the two companies, but a close working relationship continued, W. G. Bagnall Ltd being involved as a subcontractor for mechanical parts, and many of the smaller shunters were still erected at Stafford. Fortunately, as it turned out for Brush, F. H. Wood, W. G. Bagnall's Chief Draughtsman, and one of its brightest young men, had been loaned as Chief Mechanical Designer, originally on secondment in 1952; he was to remain, eventually becoming Chairman and

Photo: N. E. Preedy

Above: *No 47358, still in green livery, had recently received its TOPS number when it was photographed at Gloucester Horton Road depot on 18 May 1974. Many locomotives ran in green with TOPS numbers, No 47256 being the last in green and entering Crewe Works in October 1978 for the inevitable repaint in blue.*

No 47358 was originally No D1877, when new to Tinsley in June 1965.

It then moved as follows:

3.70	Immingham
5.73	Crewe
3.93	Old Oak Common
10.93	stored
2.94	Tinsley
4.94	stored
6.94	Tinsley
10.95	Crewe.

Liveries:
BR green from new
BR blue, July 1977
Railfreight large-logo grey, January 1987
Freightliner grey, October 1996.

Managing Director of the Brush group in 1964. Wood was not only responsible for the mechanical parts design of the Ceylon and BR locomotives, but went on to play an even greater part in later designs.

As British Railways stepped up its dieselisation plans, with an announcement, late in 1958, that it hoped to eliminate

Above: *Apart from a 20-month spell at Immingham around 1968, No 47406 had almost 17 years at Finsbury Park on East Coast main line duties. New on 11 January 1963, it was eventually transferred to Gateshead on 19 August 1979, and was named Rail Riders on 10 December 1981, a crest being added on 12 November 1985. The plates were removed when it went to Immingham in May 1988, and were attached to No 47488 which is now in the Fragonset* fleet. It was painted into the original InterCity livery in October 1985, and became well-known as it travelled the network extensively. Its end came in August 1990, but not before it had become a performer on the trans-Pennine route, also regularly dragging Class 91s between Leeds and Bradford before electrification.

The locomotive is shown leaving King's Cross with a down express on 10 July 1976.

steam traction earlier then originally envisaged (this being completed exactly 10 years later, in 1968), it became increasingly obvious that more powerful general-purpose locomotives were needed. The original A, B and C classification had meanwhile been replaced by a numerical series, where Type 1 represented power ranges 750-1,000hp, Type 2 1,001-1,500hp, Type 3 1,501-1,999hp, and Type 4 2,000-2,999hp; later Type 5 was added to cover the 3,300hp 'Deltic' locomotives. In the Type 4 range, English Electric was supplying a heavy 2,000hp locomotive (later Class 40) which utilised the massive, albeit well proven, Bulleid 1Co-Co1 bogie; although a reliable machine, their weight of 133 tons, long wheelbase and almost rigid bogies were against them from day one. BR's own workshops at Derby and Crewe, in conjunction with Sulzer (engines), Crompton Parkinson (electrical equipment), and Alan West (control gear) were building a 2,300hp 1Co-Co1 diesel (later Class 44), which also used the Bulleid bogie. Although slightly more powerful than the English Electric design, all the inherent problems of weight and rigidity were still present.

The power unit for these BR-built Type 4s was the Sulzer 12LDA28A engine, a well-tried 12-cylinder, four-stroke, twin-bank engine embodying two separate crankshafts geared together to form a common output shaft. Against the single-crankshaft English Electric 'V' form design, this offered several advantages, not least a reduction in engine component stresses, and the easy ability to run the generator either faster or slower than the engine itself, by arranging the crankshaft phasing gears accordingly. In the event, in all its applications on locomotives in this country, it has been arranged with the generator running faster than the engine. However, it has the distinct disadvantage of making a more complicated, bigger and heavier engine. Nevertheless, the Swiss-built engines fitted to the original 10 locomotives (Nos D1-10) gave good service, and the 12LDA28B intercooled version of the engine, uprated to 2,500hp, was fitted to 127 subsequent locomotives (Nos D11-137, which became Class 45). These and all other Sulzer engines (except for five 'V' form engines – see Chapter 3) used by British Railways were built under licence in this country by Vickers Armstrong, at that

company's works in Barrow-in-Furness; the locomotives were built in the BR workshops at Crewe and Derby.

When BR decided to build a further 76 locomotives, the heavy workload at Crompton Parkinson meant that that company was unable to meet the required delivery dates, so an alternative electrical contractor was sought. In 1960 the contract both for electrical equipment and control gear was placed with Brush. Ordered as Nos D138-99 and D1500-13, these locomotives were to be constructed at Derby, using the same uprated Sulzer engine; delivery began in November 1961.

In 1956, the Brush Electrical Engineering Co Ltd had been absorbed into the Hawker Siddeley Group. Within that group was engine manufacturer Bristol-Siddeley, which had the sole UK manufacturing rights for the German Maybach high-speed diesel engine. This engine, the MD650, rated at 1,100hp, was being fitted in pairs to BR's Swindon-built Type 4 B-B diesel-hydraulics, and was a very compact, lightweight power unit.

Despite the advances made with Sulzer engines in the BR-built Type 4s, it was clear that greater horsepower was needed, together with a reduction in total locomotive weight, as the existing designs were unable

to equal, let alone surpass, the best performances the individual Regions' Class 8 passenger steam locomotives could deliver. All three of the evolving principal locomotive suppliers for British Railways (English Electric, Brush and the Birmingham Railway Carriage & Wagon Co — BRCW) were well aware of this, and had plans on their respective drawing boards to overcome it. Brush designed a lightweight Co-Co, using the same Commonwealth bogie as its Type 2s, but with a much lighter integral underframe and body structure, the whole providing support for the load-bearing members. To power this locomotive, Brush decided to use two of the latest Bristol-Siddeley Maybach MD655 engines, which were rated to deliver 1,440hp at 1,500rpm, and exactly the same as those being supplied in pairs to power the BR-built 'Western' class C-C diesel-hydraulics, albeit in that case rated at 1,350hp — 2,700hp for the locomotive. The twin main generators each powered three parallel-connected traction motors and the completed locomotive, known as *Falcon*, entered service with BR for evaluation purposes in September 1961, remaining the property of Brush.

With a weight in working order of 115 tons, and with 2,800hp available, Falcon was a great advance over earlier designs, and for a prototype, turned out to be extremely successful. Almost simultaneously with this development, Sulzer further uprated its engine, introducing the 12LDA28C version, rated at 2,750hp, and this was used by the BRCW in its offering. Using Associated Electrical Industries (AEI) electrical equipment, and externally looking very like the eventual Class 47, *Lion*, as it was known, had an all-up weight of 114 tons, and took to the rails in April 1962. This

was just two months after English Electric had unveiled its prototype (DP2) which, using the 'Deltic' bodyshell and mechanical parts, achieved an overall weight of 105 tons, with the latest version of the 16SRVT engine, intercooled and rated at 2,700hp.

All these prototypes were to little avail, however; through a desire to accelerate the introduction of diesel traction (and consequent run-down of steam), British Railways had seized the opportunity offered by the 2,750hp Sulzer engine, and in late 1960 formulated proposals for a Co-Co locomotive thus powered, with an all-up weight of no more than 114 tons. Only Brush was able to take this proposal on board, a course of action influenced by the order, currently being fulfilled at Loughborough, for the sets of electrical equipment needed for the 1Co-Co1 Type 4s being built at Derby. Brush agreed to amend this order, in effect cancelling the last 20 sets, and substituting equipment (much of which was common anyway) for the new locomotives. The Class 46 build was therefore terminated at locomotive No D193, and the 20 new locomotives ordered on 28 February 1961 took the numbers D1500-19, becoming the first examples of Class 47.

Above: *No 47370 is seen at the head of an empty merry-go-round train approaching Barnetby on 12 June 1981. It was delivered from Brush as No D1889 in July 1965 and allocated to Tinsley, receiving its TOPS number in February 1974. It was frequently reallocated, chiefly within the Eastern Region, as follows:*

7.65	Gateshead
9.65	Thornaby
10.65	Tinsley
10.68	Stratford
1.70	Immingham
3.86	Tinsley
7.93	stored (briefly reinstated, 8.93)
9.93	Tinsley
11.93	stored
2.94	Tinsley
3.94	Bescot
11.94	stored
1.95	Tinsley
3.96	stored
4.96	Tinsley
4.96	Crewe.

It received the following liveries:
BR green when new
BR blue, summer 1975
Railfreight large-logo grey, November 1986
Freightliner grey liveryNovember 1996.

This locomotive was fitted for multiple-working at Immingham in April 1975 along with No 47379, and the two were known as 'Pinky and Perky'. The modification was removed in July 1982. No 47370 received the unofficial name 'Thunderbird' whilst at Tinsley depot in November 1991, and is currently still active, with Freightliner.

2
Production Gets Underway

A number of lessons learned in the first-generation diesel locomotives were embodied in the Brush Type 4s, as they were initially known, not least the requirement of the early specifications for the power unit to be removable sideways. This, of course, necessitated removal of the body-sides; thus it was not possible to have a fully integral load-bearing bodyshell, and this resulted in an otherwise unnecessary increase in the size and weight of the underframe design. The requirement was the result of a desire for all the existing railway workshops to be able to remove power units, and many of the smaller ones did not have sufficient height in their erecting shops for the cranes to lift the power units high enough to clear the body-sides. Despite being of weighty construction, the Brush Type 2 underframe had its weak points, and the area at each end where the buffer beams were mounted was particularly 'under-designed', with the result that the slightest collision resulted in a bent underframe — a dropped nose, or

'Concorde', as the staff called it!

In the Class 47, leaning heavily on the lessons learned with *Falcon*, the whole of the underframe, together with the bodyshell, was redesigned as an integral load-bearing structure, and the area around the buffer beams was given considerable attention, so that buffing shocks were transmitted through the entire body — indeed it was designed to take an end-on buffing load of 200 tons. A special triangular framework was incorporated at each end, so that buffing loads were transferred to the stressed skin body-sides, which were themselves braced by a number of bulkheads acting as cross-ties. The whole body and underframe design was an advance on *Falcon*, and as a result considerably lighter. Apertures on the body-sides were kept to a minimum because of the loads they had to bear; necessary of course, to keep the weight of the members themselves as low as possible. Despite *Falcon* also having an integral load-bearing

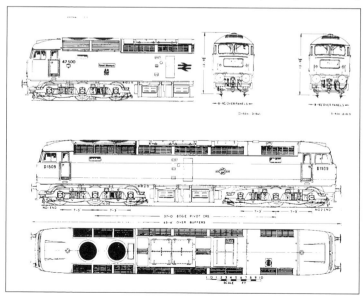

underframe and body construction, the actual body-sides took no load, but reducing the weight of the whole body was of greater importance in the new Type 4s, as the all-up engine weight was no less than 22.3 tons, compared to the 13.8 tons of two Maybachs. In all, this redesigning of the body reduced *Falcon's* 21.5 tons to 17 tons, a commendable achievement. It was also possible to reduce the overall length of the locomotive from 65ft to 59ft 10½in; the Type 2, incidentally, was 53ft 1in long, and the comparable body weight 18.4 tons.

In the redesign, all the filtration for engine, electrical machines and steam heating boiler was via filters mounted in the roof sections above cantrail level. The radiators were also roof-mounted, along with their associated cooling fans. The whole body design relied heavily on the Hawker Siddeley Aviation Division, and its developing expertise in stressed skin construction, a clear benefit of Brush's being in the Hawker Siddeley group.

The cast-steel Commonwealth bogie used on the Type 2s was to all intents and purposes identical to the one used on *Falcon* although the latter had all axles powered. However, some redesign was undertaken for the new Type 4, and this took account not only of the need to reduce weight, but also of advances in suspension design, and the use of coil springs and damping, in lieu of the leaf variety. Firstly, the elliptical leaf spring secondary suspension was replaced by nests of coil springs, hydraulic dampers

Above: *The daily Red Bank van train across the Pennines from Newcastle (Leeds on Sundays) was guaranteed, as in steam days, to provide a wide variety of motive power. On Sundays it was a much shorter train, as is shown in this picture of No 47342 approaching Sowerby Bridge station on 22 August 1982. Note the small number on the front of the cab — not unusual at this time. On the skyline is the famous local landmark 'Wainhouse Tower', believed to have been built to allow a gentleman to see into his neighbour's garden after a dispute.*

No D1823 was new to the LMR Midland Division in March 1965, and became No 47342 under TOPS. It was unfortunate to become the first '47/3' to be withdrawn, in November 1988, after an accident at Ashbury's Yard, Manchester on 19 September 1988. Its first move away from the Toton/Midland lines was on 23 November 1968 to Crewe, but it returned to Toton on 15 February 1969, moving to Bescot on 8 May 1971 and finally back to Crewe on 9 October 1971.

being used for spring damping; secondly, manganese steel was used to reduce the weight further, and thirdly a complete redesign of the brake gear resulted in a total of four brake cylinders per locomotive, against twice that number on the original design. This latter 'improvement' was at the obvious cost of much additional leverage, and has perhaps been one of the least successful of the innovations. Since new, the class has been bedevilled by bogie brake gear problems, and the general wear and tear of the brake gear has made it expensive to maintain to the necessary standards, and the 'Achilles heel' of bogie overhaul periodicities. However, the total effect of all these measures was a creditable reduction in weight, from the 27 tons of *Falcon's* bogies, to a little over 25 tons for the Class 47.

The three-per-bogie nose-suspended traction motors were four-pole force-ventilated machines, having a continuous rating of 422V and 710A, with a speed of 776rpm amounting to 368hp. To reduce overall bogie length, the trailing motor on each bogie was mounted in the opposite direction to its sisters, and as the centre axle was allowed some side play within the bogie frame, its resilient suspension link was of different design; in order to overcome side-force effects, a shock absorber was provided to 'control' the sideways movement of this

Above: *I don't know if anybody has kept a record, but I suspect that every Class 47 has visited the North Wales coast main line sometime. Crewe-based Class 47/4s worked Euston-Holyhead expresses for many years until the High Speed Trains arrived, and even in 1999 there is still a Class 47 diagram on these trains. In this picture we see No 47535 University of Leicester, so-named on 12 May 1982, approaching Penmaenbach Tunnel on the 13.45 Manchester-Bangor on 21 April 1983.*

Originally based at Cardiff Canton when new as No D1649 on 2 January 1965, the locomotive was allocated No 47065 under TOPS but never carried this, being converted to a '47/4' and thus becoming No 47535 in April 1974. It was moved frequently around the Western and Midland divisions of the London Midland Region. The other end was damaged in an accident with a DMU at Luton on 28 May 1983. It ran in plain BR blue minus logo after overhaul in December 1977, receiving the large-logo blue livery in June 1986, followed by Parcels Sector red livery in August 1990, applied at Old Oak Common depot. It was eventually switched off on 20 February 1999 at Old Oak Common after derailment damage.

Above: *No 47429 spent many years at Gateshead, and could be found all over the network. Here we see it crossing the Selby swing bridge at the head of an up relief to King's Cross on 23 September 1983. It carried BR green livery when new as No D1541 to Darnall in September 1963, followed by BR blue livery until its withdrawal in January 1987 to provide spares. It was cut up at Crewe in December 1988. Virtually its entire career was spent on the Eastern Region, the allocations being as follows:*

9.63	Darnall (new)
4.64	Tinsley
1.65	Finsbury Park
7.67	Tinsley
7.70	York
8.72	Tinsley
11.72	Gateshead
8.79	Finsbury Park
5.81	York
1.82	Gateshead
11.85	Bescot (on loan)
2.86	Gateshead
3.86	Crewe
5.86	Bescot
11.86	Inverness
1.87	withdrawn.

Its last working was to Holyhead, on 26 January 1987, and it was cut up at Crewe in December 1988.

motor. Suspension bearings were of roller bearing design, and the axlebox bearings Hoffmann parallel rollers, with bronze thrust pads to control side movement. Like the brake gear already mentioned, this type of axlebox became a problem, and with the benefit of hindsight, should not have been used. Later builds therefore had either Timken or SKF (Skefco) taper roller-bearings.

The Sulzer 12LDA28C 12-cylinder twin bank engine was a four-stroke, single-acting, direct injection pressure-charged and intercooled unit, with a rating of 2,750hp at 800rpm, the bore and stroke being 11.02in and 14.16in respectively. It drove three in-line generators, all dc machines, at a maximum speed of 1,150rpm — a ratio of 1:44 — via synchronising step-up gearing. Nearest the engine was the train heat generator, a Brush type TG160-16 Mk 1 machine with a continuous rating of 800V at 400A; next came the main traction machine, Brush type TG160-60 Mk 2, with a continuous rating of 844V at 2130A, and lastly the auxiliary generator rated at 110V and 240A, a Brush type TG69-16 Mk 1 machine.

Even before these 20 locomotives had entered service (between November 1962 and April 1963), further orders were placed, 30 being ordered on 1 January 1962, taking the numbers D1520-49, and a further 25 on 4 September 1962 — Nos D1682-1706. In the meantime, in an effort to speed up deliveries, BR decided to erect a batch in its own workshops, Crewe turning out Nos D1550-1681, with engines from Sulzer and electrical equipment from Brush, the first Crewe delivery being in January 1964. Thereafter, construction proceeded apace, with both Crewe and Loughborough turning them out weekly. Final deliveries came from Crewe in February 1967, with No D1111 making a total of 202 from that Works, and from Loughborough in May 1968, No D1961 being Brush's 310th — a grand total of 512.

There were many variations in design over this long production run. After the initial 20 it was decided to remove the provision of electrical train heating equipment (ETH) from the specification, a retrograde step as events were to prove, and the brake equipment was changed to that of Davies & Metcalfe manufacture. Actually, these 20 locomotives were always more of a hybrid type than any of the other multifarious varieties. To provide the ETH generator with a load even when the locomotive was not hauling electrically-heated coaches (and thus prevent commutator glazing), a number of the auxiliary machines ran off its output. The compressor and vacuum exhausters were 800V machines, as were the radiator fans, whilst the two traction motor blowers were 400V machines connected in series across the ETH generator. In all the later builds, these machines were standard 110V motors, except the radiator fans, which were replaced by a hydrostatic system, where an hydraulic pump mounted on the engine drove twin hydraulic motors operating the fans, the whole being designed to effect a reduction in the engine horsepower absorbed.

Commencing with No D1682 delivered in October 1963, the axle design was altered, a larger diameter axle being substituted, to eliminate possibilities of stress build-up, and subsequent crack development in the wheel seat area. Unfortunately, to maintain a standard traction motor for the fleet, this had a 'knock-on' effect, resulting in a redesign of the traction motor suspension tube, a split type replacing the original solid ones, and these split tubes caused many headaches later. At the same time the opportunity was taken to replace the Hoffmann parallel axlebox bearings with either an SKF or Timken taper type, thus eliminating the side thrust problems previously encountered.

From locomotive No D1714, delivered from Loughborough in February 1964, and No D1631 from Crewe in November the same year, the series-parallel configuration of the traction motor connections was changed to an all-parallel arrangement. This necessitated a complete redesign of the generator and control cubicle, so as to retain a standard traction motor and bogie arrangement for the entire fleet. There were two principal reasons for this major change in philosophy: firstly, to reduce the main generator voltage, and thus the possibility of flashovers; and secondly, to improve the electrical conditions in the initial period after a wheelslip situation, in avoiding the high rise in motor voltage after wheelslip. As BR gained experience of diesel traction, traction motor flashovers became a major problem, and as most of the locomotive types had a series-parallel type configuration, they all suffered to some extent. As this configuration was judged to be about the worst possible in a wheelslip situation, and as wheelslip protection was not as developed as some people thought, there was much pressure to do something — hence the decision to change the Class 47 design during production.

To offset the heavy generator construction otherwise necessary to carry the higher currents, a 12-pole machine was designed, and the weight was very commendably kept almost the same as with the original eight-pole machine. Along with this arrangement, the main generator separate field excitation system was altered, a small inductor-alternator (for amplification purposes) with two stator windings being introduced, driven by an extension of the main and auxiliary generator driveshafts. This, providing excitation current via one of its windings, combined with a small Torostat regulator, mounted on and driven by the engine governor in place of the conventional load regulator and resistors, effected a considerable reduction in weight. It also simplified the control gear, by reducing the power handled by the regulation system.

The next change was the introduction of equipment to operate air-braked trains, BR having made the decision gradually to change over from vacuum to air train braking. It was to be a long process, still not complete, but nevertheless causing an immediate need for large numbers of locomotives able to work air-braked trains. Moreover, to give the necessary operating flexibility, locomotives were needed that

Above and Right: *No 47515 entered service as No D1961, and was in fact the last Class 47 built. It went into traffic in January 1968, and was allocated to the West Coast main line pool. It became No 47515 under TOPS, and carried the name* Night Mail *between September 1986 and February 1991, being withdrawn two months later from Bath Road, Bristol. The first picture shows it climbing Miles Platting Bank out of Manchester Victoria, hauling Class 81 electric No 81018 on the diverted up 'Royal Scot' on 5 November 1983.*

No 47515 received the original InterCity livery (with BR double-arrow logos) in September 1986, retaining this until July 1989 when it received Mainline (unbranded InterCity) livery. One side was painted white at Bristol Bath Road

open day in 1991 showing the positions of internal components. It was eventually dumped at Holbeck depot where it is seen on 18 April 1992 (right).

It was allocated as follows:

1.68	LM Western Lines (new)
6.68	Crewe
7.68	Bescot
7.69	Crewe
4.71	Toton
3.72	Crewe
4.72	Toton
2.73	Crewe
10.82	Old Oak Common
5.88	Crewe
7.88	Eastfield
11.88	Bristol, Bath Road
1.91	stored
3.91	withdrawn.

could work both vacuum- and air-braked trains. Thus, from No D1758, new in May 1964, all Loughborough production was so equipped, Crewe following suit in October with No D1631. However, getting the necessary gear into an already cramped bodyshell proved difficult. An additional air compressor was needed, together with several more air reservoirs, and a host of smaller valves etc; access for maintenance became extremely difficult. Because of this, a complete redesign of the equipment room was later undertaken including a rethink of the engine cooling water system, so as to remove the need for the large coolant settling tank, which occupied considerable space. In the existing design, when the

engine was not running, the coolant drained out of the radiators into a settling tank, and this prevented freezing of the coolant in the exposed radiators during cold weather. In the redesigned system, the water remained in the radiators, saving the need for the cumbersome settling tank, but to prevent freezing it was necessary to protect the radiators, and hydraulically-operated shutters were provided at the air intakes. These shutters were operated by the same system that drove the fans, opening and closing depending on engine coolant outlet temperature, and of course, remaining closed when the engine was not running. Subsequently, as the whole fleet was fitted with dual air and vacuum braking systems,

this modification to the cooling system was also carried out, and the earlier dual brake conversions were brought into line too. Of course, a different system was needed on the initial 20 locomotives, as they had electric rather than hydraulic fan motors, and on these locomotives the shutters were air-operated. The modified air braking arrangements were first used on No D1631, ex Crewe in October 1964, No D1807 being the first one ex Loughborough in January 1965.

Last of the major modifications was a rearrangement of the boiler room to enable any of the three types of boiler/steam generator used to be fitted without structural modifications. The boilers/steam generators were the Spanner Mk IIIB, the Stone-Vapor BR4625, and the Clayton RO2500 Mk II. There was an operating requirement to restrict different boilers to particular Regions, and the advantage of the universal boiler room was that a change of boiler became much easier when locomotives were moved from Region to Region, although in practice boilers were never changed when locomotives were reallocated. This modification was introduced on locomotive No D1782 from Loughborough in October 1964, and on No D1631 from Crewe at the same time.

As well as these major changes in specification as the locomotives were being built, there were a host of smaller ones introduced at different stages in the production runs; for example, modifications to bogie brake gear to help restrain various parts of the linkage as wear took place, fitting of the Western Region AWS equipment to those members of the class allocated to that Region, and slow speed control. This latter alteration was to allow the locomotives to be used on 'merry-go-round' coal trains, enabling the locomotive to run at very slow speeds, whilst the train was either loaded or discharged, without stopping. The system took the form of a manually-operated vernier rheostat placed in the generator separate field circuit, but there were problems with drivers unable to maintain a constant speed frequently juggling the rheostat, and this led to a redesign. By this stage electronics were beginning to come into their own in traction applications, and a fully-electronic 'closed loop' system was designed, no fewer than 340 members of the class being so equipped, including those built with the earlier system and subsequently converted to the new standard. Later locomotives were fitted with other electronic equipment, including auxiliary voltage regulator systems (AVR), speed indicating equipment, field divert control and, later still, traction load regulation. These electronic systems were remarkably successful when one considers their pioneering status, and were fitted to all new members of the class, commencing with No D1758 from Brush in May 1964, and No D1842 from Crewe in May the following year.

The last two members of the fleet completed, Nos D1960 and D1961, both from Brush, were considerably delayed as they embodied yet further modifications, not least in being equipped with dual-wound auxiliary alternators instead of generators, which provided not only the locomotive auxiliary power supply, but 400kW of electrical load for train heating. By this time, BR had made a decision gradually to change over from steam to electric heating of trains, and these advances in alternator technology represented a significant saving in space and weight over the dc equipment fitted to Nos D1500-19. As events turned out, these two locomotives became the precursors of the later conversions, the Class 47/4s and 47/7s as we know them today. Because of

Above: An immaculate No 47112, complete with Stratford depot white roof, passes through Ipswich station with a down Freightliner heading for Felixstowe on 12 April 1984, not long before electrification.

This locomotive was new in January 1964 as No D1700, and received its TOPS number in February 1974.

Its allocations were as follows:

1.64	Old Oak Common (new)
2.65	Bristol, Bath Road
4.66	LM Western Lines
6.68	Bescot
5.74	Bristol, Bath Road
8.74	Bescot
10.74	Bristol, Bath Road
5.77	Cardiff Canton
3.83	Stratford
5.85	Cardiff Canton
5.87	Bristol, Bath Road
5.87	Stratford
5.89	Tinsley
7.91	Old Oak Common
11.91	withdrawn
5.97	cut up at Old Oak Common.

Delivered in BR green, it was repainted BR blue in 1971, the white roof being added 17 March 1984. It became a Railfreight Distribution locomotive in March 1987.

the nature of the modifications needed on these two locomotives, including a further modification to the load regulation system on No D1961, they were not delivered until July 1967 and May 1968 respectively, the latter 15 months after Crewe's last delivery, No D1111 of February 1967.

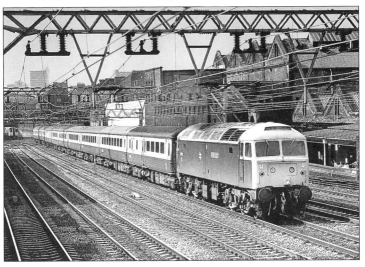

Above and Overleaf (top): Prior to the electrification of Liverpool Street-Norwich services, No 47596 Aldeburgh Festival was one of Stratford depot's regular locomotives on these duties in the early 1980s. It is shown here climbing Bethnal Green bank at the head of the 12.30 express to Norwich on 19 March 1985. Originally No D1933 when it entered service at Bristol Bath Road in March 1966 in green livery, it became No 47255 under TOPS, and was again renumbered as 47596 in September 1983. It was later allocated No 47740 in the Rail Express Systems postal series, but never carried it. The locomotive was named in June 1984.

A comparison taken 4½ years later (overleaf), on 19 August 1989, shows the same locomotive in Network SouthEast livery and with the 'Cockney Sparrow' symbol on the body-side. It is working the empty stock from the 09.00 King's Lynn-Liverpool Street back to Stratford.

Its allocations were:

3.66	Bristol, Bath Road (new)
9.72	Bescot
7.73	Tinsley
1.75	Gateshead
3.75	Holbeck
2.76	Stratford
10.80	York
5.81	Thornaby
6.81	Stratford
10.82	Gateshead
12.82	Stratford
10.87	Bristol, Bath Road
7.88	Tinsley
1.89	Stratford
3.89	Old Oak Common
3.89	Stratford
4.89	Old Oak Common
4.89	Stratford
5.90	Old Oak Common
7.91	Crewe
3.99	taken out of traffic.

The locomotive was repainted in standard BR blue by 1974, having a silver roof added on 9 July 1977, and finally receiving the revised version of Network SouthEast livery in March 1989.

Above: A Scottish locomotive for most of its working days, No 47595 Confederation of British Industry *is seen undergoing an examination inside Eastfield depot on 12 June 1985. It went new to Haymarket as No D1969 in October 1965, became No 47268 under TOPS, No 47595 on ETH conversion in September 1983, No 47675 in August 1991 and finally No 47791 for RES in October 1994.*

Its allocations were as follows:

10.65	Haymarket (new)
10.68	Crewe
10.69	Haymarket
9.76	Eastfield
6.78	Haymarket
10.83	Eastfield
3.91	Inverness
9.92	Bristol, Bath Road
5.93	Immingham
4.94	Crewe
10.98	Motherwell.

By the time the first Class 47s were under construction, the Eastern Region (ie, the original Eastern Region, before combining with the North Eastern) was well on its way to the total elimination of steam traction. Indeed, the Great Eastern section achieved this by 1963. The ER was also the most vehement Region in its criticism of existing Type 4s, claiming that at 133 tons for 2,000hp, or even 2,500hp, they were too heavy and not powerful enough to equal, let alone surpass, Class 8 steam performance. (Indeed, for this reason, it had already gained Board approval for a limited number of 3,300hp 'Deltic' locomotives, in the Type 5 power range.) However, the publicity value that BR stood to gain from having one Region completing steam replacement made the ER first choice for the allocation of the new locomotives, and thus it came about that No D1500 left Brush's Loughborough works for Finsbury Park depot in November 1962. All the initial batch of 20 locomotives started their lives at this depot, delivery being completed with No D1519 in April the following year. In the event, the next 15 went there too, arriving between June and August 1963. These deliveries effectively saw the end of steam on the Great Northern main line south of Doncaster, with the famous Top Shed at King's Cross closing its doors for the last time with the onset of the 1963 summer timetable, in June that year.

Tinsley depot in Sheffield was the recipient of the remainder of the second batch, but it was not long before locomotives started to appear on the North Eastern, Western and London Midland Regions, with each having an allocation by September 1964. The Scottish Region did not get any until the delivery of Nos D1968-72 from Crewe in November 1965, but earlier examples had been frequent visitors to both Glasgow and Edinburgh on Anglo-Scottish workings. Only the Southern Region did not get an allocation from new, although once again, there were frequent visits on inter-regional passenger and freight workings. In fact, the Southern did have an allocation for a short period, D1921-6 being allocated to Eastleigh during 1966-8, to cover duties on the South Western main line, particularly boat trains and Waterloo-Bournemouth/Weymouth expresses, after the elimination of steam, and before delivery of the converted Class 74 electro-diesel locomotives.

Before dealing with the early service experiences, it is opportune to recall a further significant modification made to a few locomotives during production. Even by late 1964, problems were beginning to develop with the Sulzer engines — of which more anon — and it was decided to try, in a small batch of locomotives, the Sulzer 'V' form engine, a more recent development than the twin crankshaft engine otherwise being fitted. This engine, series designation LVA24, had been under continuous development since 1960, already being in traction use on the French Railways. The 12-cylinder version, with a nominal rating of 3,000hp at 1,100rpm, was fitted to five locomotives being built at Loughborough, Nos D1702-6, but in this case the engine was derated to deliver 2,650hp a 1,050rpm, 100hp less than the twin-crankshaft engines.

Some internal redesign of the locomotives was necessary, and a variation of the TG160-60 generator, the Mk 5, was used, the engine running clockwise as opposed to its twin-crankshaft equivalent which, via engine phasing gears, ran anti-clockwise at its output shaft. Also, as the output shaft ran slower, 1,050rpm compared to 1,150rpm (although of course the actual engine ran faster — 1,050rpm vice 800rpm), it was necessary, so as to maintain generator output, to strengthen the self field. Otherwise, the electrical systems were identical.

These locomotives went new to Tinsley depot in Sheffield, arriving there between September 1965 and July 1966, although they were initially outbased at Shirebrook for 'merry-go-round' coal train duties, but by 1969 they had all migrated to the Great Eastern section at Stratford, where they were used on passenger workings. However, they all returned to Tinsley the following year.

Perhaps due to their being non-standard, they never seem to have been popular, despite suffering fewer engine-related problems than their sisters, but they did suffer some bearing problems. In the 1968 general reclassification of BR's diesel locomotive fleet they became Class 48, but as the twin-crankshaft engines in Class 47s began to settle down following modifications, a decision was made to convert these hybrids to standard, and this work was undertaken at Crewe between December 1969 and June 1971. By the end of 1967 each of these locomotives was credited with 8,000-9,000 hours of engine use, and all had accumulated something in the region of 115,000 miles, so a

Above: *On 23 June 1989, No 47595 is seen leaving Arbroath with the 'Devon Scot' 07.07 Plymouth-Aberdeen. It carries BR Mainline livery — basically the InterCity colours without any logo; note also the very small number applied to the lower cabside.* **47595's liveries** were:
*BR green when new
BR blue between February 1974 and April 1975
Large-logo blue, from March 1985
BR Mainline, from October 1988
RES red/grey, from October 1994.*

Below: *In 1991, a small sub-class — 47/6 — was created. Seven locomotives were modified with uprated ETH output for working sleeper trains in Scotland, and were restricted to 75mph. One of these was No 47675, which retained its* name Confederation of British Industry. *Here it is seen on 26 March 1992 shunting timber wagons at Keith, probably as a fill-in turn between its sleeper duties.*

After its time in Scotland it spent a couple of years on Infrastructure duties. It was damaged by fire in February 1994, being restored to main line order for RES as No 47791 in October 1994 and renamed Venice Simplon Orient Express in 1995. By 1999 it was back in the Scottish sleeper pool.

heavy engine overhaul was becoming due in any case. As events turned out, the engines were resold to Sulzer Bros, overhauled in Switzerland, and reused in French (SNCF) locomotives.

Despite much test running of the 12LDA28C engine at 2,750hp, and extensive experience with No D57, the last of the Class 45s delivered (ex Crewe in July 1963), which had had its type 'B' engine uprated to deliver 2,750hp, problems soon developed as the Class 47s accumulated the miles. D57's engine still ran at 750rpm, although the production type 'C' engines, as we have seen, ran faster at 800rpm. A type 'C' engine had successfully completed a UIC (Union International Chemins de Fer) 100-hour type-test too. The first problems were crankcase fractures, and indeed these had already appeared on the type 'B' engines fitted to the Class 45s; the cracks were in the welds where the cast steel cross-members were joined, or in the gusset plate/side wall interface. There were a number of other weld failures, the cause of which was clouded by some substandard welding, but soon fractures started to appear in the steel castings themselves. A remedy seemed to lie in a redesign of the gusset plates, and this was undertaken retrospectively in the Class 46 engines, and on 184 crankcases of Class 47 engines already in service, as well as being incorporated in future construction.

Whilst this cured the immediate problems, there was still concern, as other fractures were appearing in the cross-girders and the 'A' frame girders adjacent to the crankshaft's No 7 main bearing, and, later still, cracks appeared on some engines in the lubricating oil sumps, and in the internal coolant pipes. Whilst the girders could be repaired in BR workshops, and without on-line failures, as they were generally discovered on examination, the latter two faults were more serious, as both could cause failure, either by loss of sump oil, or its dilution with coolant. It took a long time to discover the cause of the fractures, but extensive tests on No D1733 by the Research Department established resonance in the thrust-bearing cross-girder as the principal cause; that is a pulsating torque, itself a result of crankshaft-end thrust forces. Meantime, availability of the fleet slumped to 75% against a target of 90%,

and something had to be done, and quickly.

There was considerable deliberation before a remedy was decided upon, and not a few tests, but initially, to help contain the problem, the engine speed was reduced to 750rpm. This was achieved by the simple expedient of inserting a sleeve on the engine speed-setting piston of the governor, a job taking but a few minutes, and one the owning depots could easily perform. This had the effect of lowering horsepower to 2,580, and reducing the stresses in the critical areas by some 10%. The engines of all locomotives in service were dealt with between February and April 1966. Further long-term solutions followed, and consisted of:

1 — Increased crankshaft end-float from 0.2mm to between 1.0mm and 1.22mm. This was effected by replacing the crankshaft No 1 end float bearings with ones allowing the greater clearance. It was undertaken as quickly as replacement bearings became available, at both Works, and occasionally, to speed up the operation, at depots.

2 — Alteration of the relative angle between the two crankshafts. This had the effect of reducing the unbalanced forces between the two shafts, and a reduction of 16% stress was achieved. It also altered the firing order of 'B' bank cylinders, as 'B' crankshaft was moved in its relative position to 'A' crankshaft.

3 — Larger balance-weights on the crank webs, giving a more suitable balancing ratio, and a further 12.5% reduction in stress.

4 — Strengthening of the engine sump.

Whilst item 1, together with the reduction in engine speed, was considered but a temporary measure, and was undertaken quickly at depots and Works to stem the deteriorating availability and reliability of the class, the other modifications were far more difficult and expensive to achieve. It was therefore decided to use the 17 spare engines ordered to cover the fleet, and by this time becoming available, and mount a crash programme. Thus, Vickers Armstrong, the engine manufacturers on behalf of Sulzer Bros, set up a facility at its Barrow-in-

Above: An extremely unusual double-headed combination took place on 8 August 1985 when No 47421 visited the Keighley & Worth Valley Railway to be named The Brontës of Haworth. It ran with the line's resident English Electric shunter Vulcan, *the pair being seen at Keighley station, and also made a trip on the branch working a special passenger train on its own.*

Above: The second picture shows the locomotive when brand new as No D1520, passing through Stamford on 5 June 1963. After its initial spell at Finsbury Park, it was frequently reallocated:

10.67	Tinsley
11.67	Finsbury Park
5.68	Tinsley
9.72	Gateshead
8.79	Finsbury Park
5.80	York
10.80	Immingham
2.81	Toton
9.81	York
10.81	Gateshead
5.88	Crewe
7.88	Tinsley
3.89	Crewe
1.91	Tinsley
7.91	Crewe
9.91	withdrawn
3.97	cut up at Crewe.

Furness works to receive locomotives, removing, modifying and refitting engines at a very rapid rate. Additionally, Crewe was to modify any engines of locomotives received there either for repairs or overhaul. The programme started with the modification of the 17 spare engines, the first locomotive emerging from Barrow with its engine modified on 7 April 1966. By November 1966, no fewer than 25 locomotives were being modified at Barrow per month, but this was later slowed down when it was realised that the engine speed reduction and increased crankshaft end-float were between them reducing the rate of failure considerably, and containing the problem without the more extensive, and expensive, modifications. Therefore, despite the strongly-felt need to continue with the more extensive modifications, it was decided

P. H. Wells

Above: No D1859 was new in August 1965 and allocated to Crewe, being employed on both passenger and freight duties on the West Coast main line. It is seen when only 11 months old on 2 July 1966, heading south out of Carlisle past the old Upperby steam shed, which is behind the train. It became No 47209 in February 1974, and spent several years working in Scotland. Along with Nos 47004, 47152, 47206 and 47210, it was one of the last Class 47s in Scotland to have an operable boiler, this being isolated in October 1987. The locomotive eventually joined the Freightliner fleet, where it is currently still active.

Below: To commemorate the Silver Jubilee of HM Queen Elizabeth II, Stratford depot decorated two of its Class 47/0s with the Union Jack. No 47163 is shown at the depot on 31 July 1977. This locomotive has had at least five changes of livery (including the version shown), and has carried five different numbers, starting with D1757 on entering service at Landore in August 1964. Having lost BR green for BR blue, it became No 47163 under TOPS in February 1974. In April 1984 it was renumbered 47610, retaining standard blue livery until 1988, when it received InterCity 'Swallow' livery and became No 47823. Finally it joined the Rail Express Systems fleet as No 47787, named Victim Support, and gained RES red/grey.

The locomotive was involved in an accident at Willesden around Christmas 1977, when it wrote off Class 83 No 83004 and spent the next 18 months in Crewe Works.

that the time and expense of the crash programme could no longer be justified. Barrow completed its 155th locomotive in May 1967, and by June 190 engines had been modified there, along with 111 at Crewe, making 301 in all. Thereafter, all others were modified by Crewe during the course of scheduled overhauls, with the crankshafts being re-machined and fitted with the new balance-weights at Barrow, on an exchange basis. This allowed the 17 spare engines to go back into the float and enabled Crewe to turn round classified overhauls of locomotives at the originally intended rate. Obviously, as the engine took longer to overhaul than the rest of the locomotive, without the spare float the whole programme was considerably delayed.

Despite the original intention to restore engines to 2,750hp and reduce crankshaft end-float once all modifications were completed, neither has ever been done. So, although the Class 47 is still officially regarded as a 2,750hp locomotive, all engines are set to deliver 2,580hp after each successive overhaul.

Notwithstanding these quite major early problems, and many others still to be described, the class gave commendable performances when all was well. The locomotives very soon developed a niche for themselves in both passenger and freight working, and indeed, some were delivered without steam heating apparatus, being intended solely for goods and mineral trains. These latter were Nos D1782-1836 (later 47301-55) and D1875-1900 (later 47356-81). On delivery the class was painted in a pleasing two-tone green, with red buffer beams, small yellow warning panels and black bogies and running gear. However, towards the end of the production run the decision was taken to adopt

a universal livery of blue for all BR locomotives, and the last few members of the class delivered from the Brush works at Loughborough, Nos D1953-61, were thus adorned from new. One other locomotive had been delivered in blue, No D1733 in May 1964, as a part of the BR XP64 prototype train set, but in that case the shade was slightly lighter.

Above: At the head of the 11.41 Manchester-Hull, class pioneer No 47401 rushes past Class 31 No 31302 on a ballast train at Grindleford on 2 April 1986. Happily the Class 47 is now preserved at the Midland Railway Centre at Butterley.

It was 28 September 1962 when the then No D1500 arrived at Finsbury Park, and settled down to around nine years of East Coast main line work, which included time at Darnall and Tinsley. It then had a spell of just over three years at Immingham before being based at Gateshead for nine years, when it was used frequently on trans-Pennine duties.

It then went back to Immingham for four years, where it received special treatment, being painted in a two-tone green livery and usually kept on light duties, finally being withdrawn in June 1992. Whilst at Gateshead it was given the name North Eastern, which it carried from 16 December 1981 to May 1988. Immingham later named it Star of the East, which it carried from May 1991 until withdrawal. It passed into preservation and is now owned by the 47401 Project and based at Butterley. Currently it is undergoing a major overhaul, but should be back in action in the near future.

4

Living with the Class 47s

Photo: Brush Engineering/Ian Allan Library

Above: *An undated photograph taken by Brush Engineering of No D1500 at the company's Loughborough works, presumably just before the locomotive* was delivered to Finsbury Park in September 1962.
Brush Engineering/Ian Allan Library

My first personal experience of the Class 47s, or 'Brush/Sulzers' as we then called them, was in late 1964, when the first members of the class were allocated to Crewe. Although on the Crewe North allocation (5A), actual maintenance and repair work, except the smaller 'A' examinations and minor repairs, were undertaken at Crewe Diesel depot, a function this depot undertook for all the sheds on the Western Lines of the London Midland Region. The first batches of these locomotives to be allocated to the LMR were Nos D1616-35 and D1842-61, all ex Crewe Works, the former between September and December 1964, and the latter between January and May 1965; they were later joined by Nos D1939-61 from Brush, delivery starting in April 1966. The allocation was divided between Crewe and Toton depots.

An early problem not already outlined, and one that still plagues the class, is coolant leakage, not just from the hose-pipe connections, but also the cylinder head to cylinder block transition seals, and the cylinder liner to block joint. Coolant problems generally have been, and still are, a constant source of trouble with diesel traction on Britain's railways, and to prevent both corrosion and cavitation of the internal waterways, various water treatments have been tried. By the time the Class 47s came into general service, the expensive lesson of using some form of water treatment had been learned in principle, so the class had treated water as a coolant from new, although there were regional variations.

The problems with coolant leaking were manifold, and the standard Borax-Sodium Metasilicate (BSM) mixture seemed to aggravate the situation. If the cylinder head transition rubbers leaked, it became necessary to remove the cylinder head, or heads, and if it was the liner to block joint which leaked, the pistons and liners too — both time-consuming and awkward jobs, especially with the power unit in the locomotive. Various types of transition rubber have been used, with or without a protecting outer band, and with or without an internal

Above: *Looking immaculate with its clean white roof, No 47363 waits for its next duty in the yard at Parkstone on 13 April 1984. The white roofs were the hallmark of Stratford depot in East London, which always seemed to keep its locomotives in excellent external condition. Other Class 47/3s to receive this treatment were Nos 47310, 47311 and 47328.*

Originally No D1882, the locomotive shown entered traffic at Immingham in August 1965, and then moved on as follows:

10.65	Tinsley
10.68	Immingham
7.72	Tinsley
10.72	Immingham
10.73	Thornaby
1.80	Stratford
6.81	Thornaby
5.82	Stratford
5.84	Thornaby
9.90	Tinsley
3.98	Bescot, where it is currently awaiting formal withdrawal.

It carried the following liveries:
BR green, when new
BR blue, by 1974
Railfreight, from October 1985 (with red stripe added on body-side only, from June 1987)
Railfreight grey in November 1991.

It was renumbered 47385 on 12 July 1984, reverting to 47363 on 16 October 1995

Right: No 47484 Isambard Kingdom Brunel became one of the best known Class 47s after it was selected as one of four to be repainted in Brunswick green livery for the Great Western 150th Anniversary celebrations in 1985. It is seen here at Crewe Diesel depot, having worked from Cardiff, on 1 June 1985.

As No D1662, No 47484 started life in February 1965 allocated to Landore, and moved between the Western Region's main depots until it joined the Old Oak Common allocation on 16 May 1982, where it stayed almost until withdrawal. After Nos 47079, 47500 and 47628 lost the special green livery and moved away from the WR, No 47484 stayed at Old Oak Common and became the depot's special engine, lasting in service much longer than originally intended, notwithstanding periods in store. It was finally allocated to Immingham, where it did little work in 1998, but was exhibited at the Toton open day in 1999, eventually returning to Immingham where it gave up its good bogies to a RES machine. It is thought that this locomotive is being considered for preservation at the National Railway Museum.

Right: Looking immaculate in ScotRail livery, No 47706 Strathclyde stands on Crewe diesel depot on 1 June 1985 after a visit to the Works; No 47420 is behind.

No 47706 entered service as a Western Region locomotive at Cardiff Canton as No D1936 in March 1966, and received its original TOPS number of 47494 in February 1974. In June 1979 it was converted for push-pull operation, being renumbered 47706 and reclassified Class 47/7. Along with other members of this sub-class, it put in around 11 years' hard work on Glasgow-Edinburgh/Aberdeen services, before being replaced by Class 158 units. It was then sent south to Old Oak Common to help replace the Class 50s on Waterloo-Exeter services, but never received a repaint into Network SouthEast livery. It was finally withdrawn on 21 April 1995 and sent for scrapping in August.

Left: No 47083 Orion was one of the 18 that were named by the Western region when they entered service in early 1965. Orion was originally No D1668 and was allocated to Cardiff Canton when new; it spent 21 years on the Region, shared between Bristol, Cardiff and Landore depots.

This picture was taken at Doncaster depot on 5 March 1985, when Orion was a Bristol Bath Road locomotive in standard blue livery, which it had received by June 1973.

On 12 January 1986 it moved to Eastfield, Glasgow for one week before moving on to Inverness. It received large-logo blue livery with that depot's 'Highland Stag' emblem, and was renumbered 47633. It eventually returned to Eastfield, where the 'West Highland Terrier' logo was substituted, before being withdrawn in April 1991.

Above: A fine sight at Inverness on 19 April 1986, as two Scottish loco-motives, both fitted with snowploughs, prepare to leave with trains for the south.

On the left is No 47617 University of Stirling , bearing Eastfield's 'West Highland Terrier' logo, ready to leave on the 12.30 to Edinburgh. This locomotive was numbered D1742 when new to Cardiff Canton in May 1964. It was then allocated around the network as follows:

11.65	Bristol, Bath Road
11.67	LM Western Lines
6.68	Crewe
10.68	Toton
2.69	Crewe
11.69	Bescot
5.78	Eastfield
2.79	Laira
2.79	Eastfield
5.87	Inverness
11.88	Eastfield
3.91	Inverness
9.92	Bristol, Bath Road
4.93	Crewe
5.93	Bristol, Bath Road
3.94	Immingham
4.96	stored
1.98	withdrawn.

Delivered in BR green, it is believed to have received standard BR blue in May 1972, large-logo blue in September 1984 and finally InterCity livery in February 1990. Under the TOPS renumbering scheme, it

became No 47149 in February 1974, and later 47617 (July 1984) and 47677 (July 1991).

On the right of the picture is recently ex works No 47467, at the head of the 14.30 to Glasgow. This loco entered traffic as No D1593 in June1964, acquiring its TOPS identity in November 1973. It had few livery changes, its original BR green being replaced in March 1969 by standard BR blue, succeeded in March 1985 by large-logo blue. It became the last loco (excluding preserved traction) to run for Railtrack in this livery.

Its allocations were:

6.64	Cardiff Canton (new)
11.64	Landore
4.66	Old Oak Common
9.66	Landore
1.67	Cardiff Canton
2.70	Landore
6.70	Cardiff Canton
10.71	Bristol, Bath Road
5.74	Eastfield
9.80	Inverness
10.84	Eastfield
12.84	Inverness
3.89	Eastfield
6.90	Crewe
3.98	Immingham
12.98	withdrawn and sent to Springs Branch, Wigan, for dismantling.

Above: *An empty stock movement for the Venice-Simplon 'Orient Express' is shown passing Goose Hill Junction, Normanton, on 27 June 1986, when the Midland main line was still connected. The train was en route to Bradford. No 47460 was a rather surprising choice of motive power as it was allocated to Inverness at the time — note the snowploughs which are fitted.*

No 47460 was new to Gateshead as No D1580 in May 1964, becoming No 47460 under TOPS. During its time at Stratford on Great Eastern duties, it was unofficially named 'Great Eastern', by 4 April 1978. An unofficial nameplate made from mounting car registration letters on a wooden board, silver on black. This was removed by order of BRB, April 1978. It carried BR green from new until April 1970 when it received BR blue, a silver roof being added in March 1978; it reverted to standard BR blue in April 1981, and finally gained large-logo blue in October 1985.

Depot allocations were:

5.64	Gateshead (new)
10.68	Haymarket
10.69	Immingham
5.71	Stratford
8.72	Gateshead
9.73	Holbeck
10.77	Stratford
5.78	York
1.79	Immingham
7.79	Haymarket
5.82	Eastfield
5.83	Inverness
10.90	Crewe
1.91	stored
1.91	Tinsley
7.91	Crewe
1.92	withdrawn
2.92	reinstated at Crewe
2.92	withdrawn.

metal guide. Several compositions of rubber and neophrene have been utilised, and several adhesives. A complicated and expensive spring-loaded 'Dowty' type seal was used at one stage, with some success, but the present answer is a metal bush with Nitrile top and bottom mating seals. This type has the added advantage that by varying the thickness of the metal bush, it can accommodate the different clearances between cylinder head and block, brought about by remachining of the block, as a part of the reclamation process at life extension. Although by no means the complete answer, it is much less of a problem now than it has been. Likewise, several different types of seals and sealant have been used for the cylinder liner/block interface, but they still leak occasionally. Of course, it is rare for these types of leak to cause a locomotive to fail in service, although it is by no means unknown, as they generally 'take up' when

Above: Looking immaculate in large-logo blue livery, No 47645 is shown leaving Llandudno Junction with the up Irish Mail on 19 September 1986.

The locomotive started its days at Landore depot as No D1659 in February 1965, becoming No 47075 in March 1974, and then No 47645 in March 1986. In May 1986 it was named Robert F. Fairlie in a ceremony at Blaenau Ffestiniog. It was withdrawn in February 1990 after serious fire damage during 1989.

Above: No 47379 is shown at Healey Mills yard on 19 August 1986, painted in large-logo grey Railfreight livery. It emerged from the Brush works in August 1965 as D1898 and went to Immingham depot in BR green livery, later donning BR blue, before gaining the colours seen here. It was employed on oil trains, being given the name Total Energy in April 1986, and was painted in Railfreight Petroleum livery by May 1989. It later passed to Railfreight Distribution, and on to EWS.

Its allocations were as follows:

8.65	Immingham (new)
9.67	Tinsley
7.70	Immingham
5.84	Cardiff Canton
11.84	Tinsley
3.86	Immingham
5.93	Tinsley
3.94	Immingham
3.94	stored
9.95	Tinsley
4.96	stored
5.96	Tinsley
3.98	Bescot.

Above: *Having been ousted from its King's Lynn duties on the Great Eastern lines, No 47583* County of Hertfordshire *was transferred to Old Oak Common depot for use on Paddington-Newbury commuter services, and other Western Region passenger duties. Still in the first version of the Network SouthEast livery, it awaits departure from Paddington on 17 September 1988.*

This locomotive arrived at Tinsley depot when new from Brush in October 1964 as No D1767, becoming No 47172 under TOPS on 23 March 1974; it was renumbered 47583 during November 1980, and finally 47734 on 27 March 1996. It has been reallocated no fewer than 19 times, as follows:

2.65	Stratford
6.65	Tinsley
7.65	Holbeck
8.66	Gateshead
10.67	Finsbury Park
10.69	York
11.69	Tinsley
3.70	Finsbury Park
7.70	Immingham
4.72	Gateshead
6.72	Immingham
5.75	Stratford
10.77	Immingham
5.78	Stratford
10.87	Old Oak Common
3.89	Stratford
3.89	Old Oak Common
3.93	Eastleigh
5.93	Crewe.

It also received several liveries (some non-standard):

BR green, from new
BR standard blue, by 1973
BR blue with silver roof, from October 1978
BR standard blue, from November 1980
BR blue with silver roof, from March 1981
Large-logo blue with extended white stripes on body-side, from July 1981, with added red and blue stripes on BR arrow logo from August 1981 (removed October 1981)
Extended stripes restored, January 1982
BR standard blue, from May 1984
BR blue with silver roof, from 27 September 1984
Network SouthEast (original version), from 1 August 1986
Network SouthEast (revised version), from 21 October 1989
RES, from April 1993.

Above: The Sunday morning Leeds–Red Bank vans was well known for providing unusual motive power, but the sight of No 47079 G. J. Churchward *in its Great Western green livery was quite an occasion. The train is shown passing the site of Horbury & Ossett station, which closed on 18 June 1962.*

The locomotive was new to Landore depot in February 1965 and numbered D1664. It was named George Jackson Churchward, *which was the longest nameplate carried by a BR locomotive, but this was shortened to* G. J. Churchward *in March 1979. It is shown carrying the shorter nameplate, and the crest fitted for the GWR 150 celebrations in 1985. It put in 25 years on the Western Region before being transferred to Tinsley in 1990. Its later allocations can be summarised thus:*

12.90	Tinsley
6.92	stored
9.92	Stratford
11.93	stored
2.94	Tinsley
3.94	Bescot
11.94	stored
1.95	Tinsley
3.96	stored
4.96	Tinsley
5.96	Crewe
8.96	stored
11.96	Crewe.

After it had lost its original BR green for BR blue, its name made it an obvious choice for inclusion in the 1985 GWR 150 celebrations, and it was thus repainted Brunswick Green and given GWR crests and cast number plates. Sadly it lost these, and its name, when it became the first Class 47 to be painted in the revised Railfreight livery of two-tone grey; the initial Metals sub-sector markings were changed for those appropriate to Construction, and later Distribution, upon transfer to Tinsley. It is now a Freightliner locomotive, and is currently being converted to a Class 57, through the installation of a General Motors power unit at Brush's Loughborough works; once this has been completed it should emerge as No 57009, back once more in a green livery.

the engines get towards their working temperature. Drivers are well-versed in checking the coolant level in the locomotive header tanks before leaving the shed, and having them topped up if there has been any significant 'leaking' during periods of shutdown.

The hoses themselves are another source of leakage, and as well as trying all sorts of hose material and sealant, along with stronger 'jubilee' clips, some of which allow use of a spanner to tighten them rather than just a screwdriver, they remain a problem. At one stage, a 'Smith & Johnson' flexible metal connection was used, but it was by no means the answer, being no more successful than a conventional hose. The current practice is to use a Nitrile hose, and spanner type 'jubilee' clips.

Another problem source was the coolant outlet rail, originally in two parts, one serving eight cylinder heads, and the other four, the two sections being bolted together on top of the engine. This rail took the coolant back to the radiator after it had passed through the engine. The rails used to fracture, normally where the flange connecting to the cylinder head met the upward branch pipe, but sometimes where the upward branch pipe joined the rail itself. The final answer was a

Above: No D1857 (later 47207) was allocated to Crewe diesel depot when it entered service in August 1965. At the time of this picture, 2 March 1987, it was based at Eastfield depot, as indicated by the small scottie dog logo on the side. It was well away from home as it pulled out of Severn Tunnel Junction yard on a Speedlink working.

Its allocations were as follows:

Up to 1.70 Crewe/LM Western Lines

1.70	Toton
4.70	Crewe
5.70	Toton
4.71	Crewe
5.74	Eastfield
6.75	Haymarket
1.76	Eastfield
5.79	Haymarket
2.80	Eastfield
1.82	stored
1.86	Bristol, Bath Road
10.87	Tinsley
7.92	stored
9.92	Tinsley
3.94	Bescot
11.94	stored
5.95	Bescot
5.95	Tinsley
3.96	stored
4.96	Tinsley
8.96	Crewe
8.96	stored
11.96	Crewe.

It carried the following liveries:
BR green
BR blue
Railfreight Distribution (original livery)
Railfreight Distribution (revised livery)
Freightliner.

It was named Bulmers of Hereford on 1 December 1987, but the plates had been removed by March 1994. It was named again on 27 April 1998, as The Felixstowe Partnership.

Rigth: This view was taken on 29 April 1989 at the old steam shed at Holyhead, and shows No 47637 Springburn in the first InterCity livery. This locomotive was one of nine allocated to Haymarket depot when new in November 1965. It was originally No D1976, becoming No 47274 under TOPS in September 1974. It was renumbered 47637 in January 1986, and carried the name Springburn between June 1987 and November 1989. It was a Scottish locomotive for no less than 22 years, before joining the InterCity 'long-range' fleet as 47826 in July 1989. It was the only Class 47 to have the later InterCity emblem applied to the first InterCity livery, after 'ScotRail' was removed in August 1989. It is currently still hard at work for Virgin Cross Country.*

In the background is No 47525, with its headcode panel painted all-yellow, which was a feature of this locomotive during this period.

Above: No 47522 is shown in its unique apple green livery at the head of the 11.30 Newcastle-Liverpool trans-Pennine express, at Heaton Lodge Junction, just west of Mirfield, on 7 May 1989. This locomotive was originally No D1105, and was one of the last batch of 12 to be built by Crewe in the latter half of 1966. It was allocated to York and settled down to many years' hard work on the East Coast main line. While at Stratford around 1980 it received a silver roof, but by 1983 was back in standard BR blue. It was selected for special livery treatment for the 1987 Doncaster Works open day, when the blue was exchanged for LNER apple green, and it was named Doncaster Enterprise. It carried the special livery until around June 1990, when it was painted into Parcels livery, which it retained until withdrawn on 12 December 1998.

The locomotive was involved in two accidents. The first occurred at Forteviot on 4 May 1982, when it is believed to have hit a tractor on a farm crossing at high speed. It was stored at Perth until sent to Crewe for repair. The other accident was at Dover; during repairs it received the cab from withdrawn No 47645, which gave it back an indented headcode panel, a flush front having been fitted after the 1982 crash.

Right: *A very rare working for Petroleum sub-sector Class 47/3 No 47368* Neritidae *as it finds itself at the head of the 16.55 Dyce to Glasgow Queen Street push-pull set on 23 June 1989. It is seen during a stop at Portleven station, south of Aberdeen.*

A well-travelled locomotive, it was new to Immingham in August 1965 as No D1887, and then reallocated as follows:

9.67	Tinsley
10.72	Immingham
9.73	Tinsley
5.74	Crewe, then Tinsley
6.77	Thornaby
1.80	Stratford
2.80	Thornaby
5.86	Tinsley
11.86	Cardiff Canton
6.88	Crewe
5.91	Immingham
1.93	stored
2.93	Immingham, then stored
3.93	Crewe
5.93	Bristol, Bath Road
3.94	Stratford
4.95	stored
8.95	Stratford
9.95	stored
4.96	Stratford, then stored.

It carried the following liveries:
BR green from new
BR blue, believed to October 1972
Railfreight large logo
Railfreight Petroleum from September 1988
Railfreight no logo from September 1994

Below: *At the time of this picture, taken at Holyhead on 31 August 1989, No 47483 was part of the Crewe InterCity pool. Since entering traffic on 7 December 1964, it has led a nomadic life, being allocated to the Western, London Midland and Eastern Regions at various times. It started at Cardiff Canton as No D1637 and remained on the Western Region until May 1977. It is seen* in InterCity livery without branding, and with extremely small numbers at the base of the cab. It was eventually withdrawn on 11 June 1993.

Behind is No 47632 which had failed after arriving earlier in the day on a Freightliner, and was being returned in a Holyhead-Euston express for repair at Crewe.

Above: Almost as far north as you were likely to see a Class 47, No 47469 is passing Dingwall on 17 September 1987 having been to rescue Class 37/0 No 37260 Radio Highland, which had been derailed at the junction and ended up in a field. The Class 47 was numbered D1595 when it entered traffic in June 1964, and became 47469 on 16 February 1974 under TOPS. BR green livery was replaced in August 1968 by BR blue with cabside numbers, standard BR blue being applied in June 1972. The Eastfield 'West Highland Terrier' emblem appeared on 27 May 1985, and in June 1986 the locomotive was painted in InterCity livery with ScotRail logos. It had been allocated to most of the Western Region depots by May 1974, when it went to Scotland, and shared its time between Haymarket, Eastfield and Inverness. It met a premature end when hit by runaway Class 37 No 37420 at Millerhill on 26 January 1989; it was stored and withdrawn on 19 March 1989, after donating parts to No 47477.

redesign of the rail, relieving the stresses by replacing it with sections having seven and five legs; this obviated much of the problem, but rails still occasionally fracture. Other sources of water leaks were the cylinder head core plugs, and cracks often started to penetrate from the threads in the cylinder heads. The eventual cure in this case was a redesign of the cylinder head, with much of the stress relieved from around the core plug hole. The radiator elements presented another problem area, particularly the joining face between element and manifold, and especially as they got older and the mating surfaces became pitted.

I could go on at length on the subject of coolant leakage, but I think I have outlined enough to give a flavour of the enormous problem it has been over the years, and of what has been achieved in preventing or containing it. As soon as one problem area seemed under control, another cropped up, but coolant-related on-line failures are now somewhat rare; at this stage in the locomotives' lives, it is doubtful whether much will be done to reduce them further, unless significant improvements can be achieved for a comparatively small financial outlay.

Another early problem I recall was the exhaust pipe joints. Although the earlier locomotives using the Sulzer engines seem to have survived with them, the soft, wire-impregnated gaskets had an extremely short 'tenure of office' at 2,750hp! They had to be renewed with amazing frequency, and it was a dirty and (if the locomotive was just off a job) hot task. This was especially so, of course, because a blowing exhaust joint naturally made for a dirty engine. Due to the twin vertical configuration of the engine, the exhaust pipes were placed on top of the cylinder heads. It was not, therefore, possible

to renew individual joints, as was often the case on a 'V' form engine, so complete sections of the exhaust pipe had to be removed, even if only one joint was blowing. All 12 head joints were susceptible to blowing, as well as those that joined individual sections of pipe together, and where they connected to the diffuser ring, which was where the four sections fed their combined exhaust gases into the turbocharger. Cutting replacement joints from sheets of this material (heavily impregnated with wire) was generally accompanied by bleeding fingers and much bad language! Eventually, in an attempt to overcome the problem, steel joining plates with 'Metaflex' inserts were used, but because these were thicker than the soft joints, it was necessary to place distance pieces between the turbocharger and its mounting-block, so as to lift it high enough to match the exhaust pipes.

The 'Metaflex' joints were much more successful, and eventually found their way into all the other Sulzer engines. This is not to say, however, that exhaust problems were to go away — far from it — and these are still responsible for significantly reduced availability. Several other modifications have been tried over the years, and currently completely new pipes are fitted, with flexible bellows, in an effort to ease the problem of expansion and contraction. A lot of problems have occurred with the parallel pipe connecting flanges, which allow for expansion on the normal arrangement, especially when odd sections of new pipe have been fitted, and it is difficult to get a good fit of the expansion flanges between old and new pipes. Broken studs are another problem, both at cylinder head and turbocharger interface, and various materials have been used for the studs and bolts in attempts to cure this. Even the 'Metaflex'

Above: A trio of differently-liveried Class 47s is seen lined up at Doncaster depot on 21 September 1989.

On the right is the first of the Class 47/3 non-boilered locomotives, No 47301, which at the time was allocated to Thornaby and in Railfreight 'red stripe' livery, with some added Thornaby embellishments. It was new to Tinsley as No D1782 in November 1964.

Next in line is No 47238 in the original Railfreight Distribution livery, which was applied from 1987. It was new to Cardiff Canton depot as No D1915 in December 1965. It carries the name Bescot Yard, which

it received in October 1988.

On the left of the picture is No 47836, in the final InterCity livery. This locomotive has had many identities. It was new to Landore as No D1609 in August 1964, adopting the number 47030 in December 1973; in September 1984 it was renumbered 47618, and the following month received the name Fair Rosamund previously carried by No 47510, retaining this until September 1989. At this point it became No 47836, but reverted to No 47618 in April 1993. More recently it has joined the RES fleet as No 47780.

Above: Recently repainted into the very drab plain grey departmental livery, No 47353 poses for the camera on Holbeck depot, Leeds, between duties on 3 July 1990.

Originally No D1834, this locomotive entered traffic on the LMR Midland Division in March 1965, and no doubt spent most of its time on coal trains.

It was new in BR green, and received BR blue livery in the early 1970s. The plain grey Departmental livery was applied in January 1990, and the second version (with yellow relief) by January 1992; finally, in February 1998 it received Freightliner livery, which it still carries.

Above: *Two Parcels Sector-liveried Class 47/4s, No 47575* City of Hereford *and No 47458* County of Cambridgeshire, *make a colourful sight at Bolton, where they had arrived on 26 May 1992 to work the evening mail trains.*

City of Hereford *was named in June 1985. It started its career as No D1770 at Tinsley, becoming No 47175 in February 1974, and 47575 in June 1981. At this stage it was still running in BR blue (which had inevitably replaced its original green), but differed from the others in having the yellow front extended to the back of the cabs, and larger than normal numbers. It was painted into Parcels Sector livery in September 1990, and was to have joined the RES fleet as No 47730, but this did not happen. It is currently (May 1999) still active, but unlikely to last much longer.*

No 47458 entered service at Gateshead depot in February 1964 as No D1578, assuming its TOPS identity in February 1974. By May 1972 BR standard blue had replaced the original green, but was embellished in March 1978 with a silver roof, red buffer beams and white piping; some of these features lasted until repaint into large-logo blue in October 1986. It spent most of its days on the Eastern Region, with five months at Eastfield in May 1988, before arriving at Bristol, Bath Road, in May 1989. It was painted in Parcels Sector livery following fire damage repairs at Crewe in September 1990; indeed, it seems to have been rather accident-prone, having earlier sustained damage in October 1982, and again at Cambridge in October 1984. In December 1990 it received the name County of Cambridgeshire, previously carried by No 47585. Withdrawn on 27 May 1993, it was towed away from Holbeck depot to Booth's of Rotherham on 2 February 1996, for scrapping.

joints themselves still blow occasionally.

Other engine-related problems included incidences of high crankcase pressure, to some extent a result of ignorance on the part of the maintenance staff, in not cleaning out the exhaust venturi valve correctly. But the frequency of its needing such attention was much greater than experience had indicated from the Sulzer engines in lower-powered locomotives. The principle of the crankcase ventilation system used by Sulzer is to maintain a slight negative pressure in the crankcase, with the exhaust gases on their way to atmosphere, between turbocharger and silencer, passing through a venturi valve. This valve is connected via a flame trap to the crankcase. Thus, the vacuum created by the exhaust gases on their way to atmosphere, via

Above: The very attractive ScotRail livery is seen to advantage on No 47709 as it passes Greenhill Junction with the diverted 11.25 Glasgow Queen Street-Aberdeen on 4 September 1988. This locomotive entered service as No D1942 in June 1966 on the West Coast main line division, becoming No 47499 under TOPS, and No 47709 when it was converted for push-pull operation in 1979. The name Lord Provost was carried between September 1979 and December 1990. After being ousted from Scotland by Class 158s, it was employed on Waterloo-Exeter services, receiving Network SouthEast livery in 1990. When Class 159s took over the South Western main line, it moved on again, to Rail Express Systems.

It received the following liveries:
BR green, when new
BR blue, with silver roof added by
   August 1984
ScotRail livery, June 1985
Network SouthEast (revised version),
   November 1990
Fragonset, September 1998 and still
   carried.

Its allocations were:

6.66	LM Western Lines (new)
6.66	Toton
7.66	LM Western Lines
6.68	Bescot
12.69	Crewe
11.71	Bescot
9.72	Bristol, Bath Road
5.76	Landore
5.77	Bristol, Bath Road
5.78	Laira
8.79	Haymarket
10.87	Eastfield
10.90	Old Oak Common
3.93	Eastleigh
4.93	Crewe
7.96	stored
9.97	Tyseley.

Above: Two ex works Class 47/4s, Nos 47520 and 47470, stand outside Doncaster shed in Mainline livery on 24 November 1988.

On the left is No 47520 which entered traffic as No D1103 at York in October 1966. It received its TOPS number 47520 in March 1974 and kept it for the rest of its career. It received the following liveries: BR green when new; BR blue from April 1974; Mainline from November 1988. It spent its first 20 years allocated to East Coast main line depots, as will be noted from the following :

10.66	York (new)
10.67	Holbeck
11.67	Gateshead
6.68	Thornaby
10.68	Finsbury Park
3.70	Gateshead
10.73	York
10.74	Gateshead
3.75	York
5.76	Holbeck
10.77	Gateshead
1.79	York
1.82	Gateshead
5.87	Crewe
5.92	Bristol, Bath Road
5.93	Immingham
11.94	Crewe
11.96	stored
11.96	Crewe
9.97	stored
12.97	Immingham
3.98	stored
8.98	officially withdrawn.

Its last working was on 9 April 1997, after which it was stored. It was taken to Tinsley for parts removal on 16 December 1997 and then to Booth's of Rotherham for scrapping on 16 March 1998. It was named Thunderbird on 24 November 1993 at King's Cross, due to its duties covering failures on the ECML. No 47470 started life as No D1596 in BR green in June 1964. It ran in BR blue livery until November 1988, when it received Mainline livery.

Its allocations were as follows:

6.64	Cardiff Canton (new)
11.64	Landore
6.66	Old Oak Common
10.66	Landore
5.67	Cardiff Canton
1.69	Landore
3.69	Old Oak Common
11.69	Bristol, Bath Road
5.74	Haymarket
2.77	Eastfield
5.78	Haymarket
11.79	Eastfield
2.81	Haymarket
2.82	Eastfield
11.83	Inverness
2.84	Eastfield
5.87	Inverness
6.88	Eastfield
3.91	Immingham
4.91	Crewe
9.91	stored
11.91	withdrawn
7.95	broken up by MRJ Philips at Crewe.

Left: *In its special Infrastructure livery, No 47803 powers away from Chesterfield at the head of the 17.25 York-Derby on 31 August 1993. The locomotive was originally No D1956 and entered service in blue livery, with BR double-arrow logos on both sides of each cab, and numbers at each end of the plain body-sides. It was one of the last batch of Class 47s, and was delivered from Brush to the LMR in December 1966, entering service on the West Coast main line. It was one of the most widely allocated members of the class, seeing service in most Regions, as is clear from the following:*

6.68	Crewe
7.73	Bescot
8.74	Crewe
10.74	York
2.78	Haymarket
8.79	Laira
5.81	Landore
5.82	Old Oak Common
5.84	Stratford
5.85	Bescot
9.85	Carlisle Kingmoor
5.87	Crewe
5.88	Bristol, Bath Road; then Crewe
5.92	Bristol, Bath Road (stored briefly 8.92)
9.92	Crewe
5.93	Bristol, Bath Road
3.94	Stratford
4.95	stored; many components removed by May 1999.

Liveries were as follows:
Early BR blue (as described above), from new
Standard BR blue (but numbers positioned low as per early BR blue), from October 1974
BR blue with silver roof, from November 1984
Early InterCity livery, from November 1987
Infrastructure yellow livery, from April 1993 ('Infrastructure' titles removed shortly afterwards).

It received TOPS number 47260 in February 1974, then 47553 in September 1974 and finally 47803 in March 1989. It carried the name Women's Guild, *between June 1989 and July 1992.*

Opposite Right: *Looking extremely smart in the revised Railfreight Distribution livery, No 47234 stands outside Tinsley depot on 2 October 1993. This handsome livery looked fine when clean, but unfortunately the dark blue roof soon became black, after only a short time in traffic. This locomotive was originally numbered D1911 on entering traffic in November 1965 at Cardiff Canton. Its first reallocation away from the Western Region was not until 18 July 1987, when it was transferred to Tinsley; on 19 July 1996 it moved to Crewe. It was transferred to the* Freightliner business on 26 July 1996 and is currently working in that company's original two-tone grey livery.

To summarise, liveries carried were:
BR green, from new
BR blue, by November 1973
Railfreight Distribution (original), from June 1989
Railfreight Distribution (revised), from October 1993
Freightliner, from April 1997.

Right: Basking in the sunshine outside Tinsley depot, No 47145 shows one of its many livery variations, on 4 October 1993.

When delivered in May 1964, this locomotive was numbered D1738, assuming its TOPS identity in March 1974. New to Cardiff Canton, it then moved as follows:

6.65	Bristol, Bath Road
11.67	LM Western Lines
6.68	Crewe
10.68	Toton
2.69	Crewe
11.69	Bescot
10.76	Cardiff Canton
1.77	Laira
10.77	Cardiff Canton
5.81	Laira
5.82	Cardiff Canton
5.84	Bristol, Bath Road
7.87	Tinsley
5.88	withdrawn
11.88	reinstated at Tinsley
3.98	Bescot.

BR green livery was replaced by BR blue by November 1970. Tinsley depot's 'Rose' emblem had appeared above the body-side numbers by October 1989. In June 1990 Tinsley effected a repaint in blue with yellow lower cab fronts, black window-surrounds and an orange cantrail line, and added cast depot plaques and BR double-arrow symbols (the latter later replaced by red plastic). Body-side numbers were slightly larger than normal, and the abbreviated number '145' appeared on the cab fronts as per standard RfD practice. Tinsley 'Rose' emblems, which featured between the marker lights, were later obscured by multiple-working equipment. The red/yellow Railfreight Distribution sub-sector decals had appeared on the body-sides by November 1992; these were replaced in 1993 by the General User decals shown here. By October 1994 full yellow ends and Railfreight Distribution markings had been added, and Channel Tunnel logos were applied to the cabsides before a final repaint at Tinsley in 1998, before the depot's closure.

At Tinsley on 30 September 1989, No 47145 received the unofficial name 'Jostinot', this being painted on the body-sides; on 25 May 1990 (also at Tinsley) it was renamed 'Merddin Emrys', again unofficially but using nameplates — these were removed on 30 October 1991. Its last classified repair was at Tinsley in October 1994, by which time it had accumulated 12,859 engine hours since its previous overhaul in 1983. By July 1999 it was one of the last seven former RfD Class 47s to remain in traffic, and is currently under repair at Crewe.

the venturi valve, causes a vacuum in the crankcase, the level of which can be adjusted by means of a hole in an orifice plate, mounted in the pipe between flame trap and venturi. This system had a distinct advantage over others, in that the amount of vacuum created in the crankcase varied, depending on the pressure (and by definition engine power output) of the exhaust gases. Thus, as the crankcase pressure built up with power output, so the vacuum created by the exhaust gases increased, and the crankcase depression was maintained within strict limits. (One could draw an analogy with a steam locomotive blastpipe!) Some nasty crankcase explosions in the early days, caused by blocked venturis, resulted in the fitting of 'Bicera' pressure relief valves on the crankcase doors, six per side, set to open if the pressure in the crankcase increased beyond 1psi, and these have been very successful in achieving this — so much so, that all BR's Sulzer engines were subsequently fitted.

Crankcase pressures are measured by means of a 'manometer', which can be mounted on the free end of the engine, and can be adjusted by means of the orifice plate, when engines are load-tested after overhaul. However, it is often necessary, between overhauls, to adjust these when piston blow-by increases, to keep engines in service longer. Normally, this means putting the locomotive on a static load bank, so as to simulate a full power situation, but it is not unknown to go into traffic on a locomotive, carrying in one's pocket a selection of plates with variously-sized orifices, and to change them in co-operation with the driver at stopping places, until the correct depression is achieved!

Other mechanical problems centred around the bogie, which suffered fractures, both to its main sections adjacent to the lifting brackets and horns, and the spider casting. This latter is, in effect, the secondary suspension — a large spider-shaped casting that takes the centre bogie pivot, and is mounted via large coil springs to the bolsters. These latter fractures were quite serious, complete 'legs' fracturing and resulting in the loss of a large proportion of secondary suspension all at once. The cracks were traced to a defective batch of castings, having been cast with their walls too thin, the result of some bad workmanship on the part of whoever made

the moulds; there were also, I believe, some bad castings due to impurities in the metal. A spate of horn cheek liner weld fractures also occurred, but these were not as serious as first thought, and it was not necessary (as first envisaged) to withdraw locomotives from service to repair them, rather wait until the next convenient scheduled examination.

I have already mentioned some of the problems experienced with the brake gear, but a much more serious one surfaced in the late 1960s, when it became apparent that the brake force available was seriously impaired, through a combination of worn tyres and worn brake blocks. Indeed, so serious was this, that it became necessary to measure the combined tyre and brake block together, and if not of sufficient thickness at 'A' examinations, renew the blocks irrespective of their thickness. This meant that a locomotive with minimum-sized tyres (3in when new, scrap at around 1in), would only last a few days on a set of blocks and it was necessary, in extreme cases, to throw away expensive blocks hardly used. This was, of course, far preferable to the tremendous drop in brake force otherwise, and the cure for this problem was a redesign of the brake pull rods, replacing a single pin connection to the intermediate hangers with a series of holes and set screws, so that the rods were adjustable. Thereafter, these rods could be shortened after tyre turning, so as to maintain brake force down to the normal brake block scrapping size guideline, ie a minimum of 1in at the thinnest point, at 'A' examinations. However, this was not before a lot of good brake blocks had had to be changed, and a lot of fitters became very frustrated! (It is bad enough changing these anyway, without having both to take down and put up heavy blocks!) The modification was made very quickly, and some locomotives were modified at the sheds, rather than waiting for their next visit to a Main Works.

Something had to be done, and done quickly, to combat the heavy wear and tear on the brake gear, which often got so bad that part of the brake block passed alongside the outside of the tyre, a phenomenon known as 'flanging'. Flanging brake blocks cause uneven heating of the tyre, and this can cause thermal fractures on their outer walls which, if allowed to spread (by continued

Above and Below: No 47448 was named Gateshead from May 1988 until May 1991, while mainly working the trans-Pennine services. It is seen bursting into the sunshine at Gledholt near Huddersfield on the 07.45 Newcastle-Liverpool on 22 January 1989.

A Darnall engine when new in March 1964 as No D1565, it became No 47448 under TOPS. It received BR blue livery in June 1973, followed in July 1987 by large-logo blue, which was its final livery. It was first stored in August 1990 whilst allocated to Crewe and was finally withdrawn in May 1991 and dumped at Leeds Holbeck.

It was allocated as follows:

3.64	Darnall (new)
5.64	Immingham
10.64	Stratford
1.65	March
5.68	Norwich
6.69	Immingham
3.73	Bescot
4.73	Crewe
11.86	Inverness
5.88	Crewe
8.90	stored
9.90	Crewe
11.90	stored
4.91	Crewe
5.91	stored
5.91	withdrawn.

Above: Beautifully prepared by Tinsley depot for the open weekend at Basford Hall, Crewe, No 47375 gleams under the floodlights in Basford Hall yard on 20 August 1994, ready for the thousands of visitors expected over the following two days. It received the name *Tinsley Traction Depot — Quality Approved* in February 1990, and was always kept in fine condition by the depot's staff.

The locomotive was new to Tinsley as No D1894 in December 1965, gaining its TOPS identity in February 1974. It was then allocated as follows:

2.66   Holbeck
5.66   Tinsley
7.66   Holbeck
3.67   Knottingley

10.71   Thornaby
5.72   Crewe
7.72   Thornaby
5.74   Knottingley
8.79   Healey Mills
5.80   Tinsley
3.98   Bescot
2.99   stored.

Delivered in BR green, it was later repainted in the following liveries:
BR blue, by December 1973
Railfreight Distribution (original),
   October 1989 (with silver window
   frames from January 1990)
Railfreight Distribution (revised),
August 1994.

Right: Nicely cleaned up in Railfreight Distribution livery, No 47213 is seen at the head of the first regular MOD service tank train on the reopened Wensleydale line from Redmire, on 14 February 1997. It is at Castle Hill Junction, Northallerton, waiting to join the East Coast main line. At the other end of this top-and-tail operation is No 47033 The Royal Logistics Corps.

No 47213 was originally No D1863 and entered service in May 1965 at Tinsley. It received its TOPS number in February 1974. 32 years later it was back at Tinsley as part of the Railfreight Distribution fleet. It was finally withdrawn in February 1999.

Below: The original drab plain grey Civil Engineering livery was transformed by the addition of the yellow band along the top of the body. No 47331, looking very clean, is carrying out Civil duties as it heads north past Hasland at the head of a Mountsorrell- Doncaster ballast train on the glorious afternoon of 1 May 1997.

When new from Brush in February 1965 as No D1812, this locomotive was allocated to the LMR's Midland Division. Its TOPS number appeared in May 1974. Having earlier

traded its original BR green for BR blue, it received Railfreight large-logo grey in November 1986, and the revised Departmental livery ('Dutch' yellow/grey, as illustrated) in September 1992. No 47331 was the last Civil Engineer's Class 47 to be given an overhaul, which was completed in June 1993. It was withdrawn in June 1999.

Opposite Left: One of the most striking liveries to be applied to the class was that selected by Porterbrook Leasing for two of its Class 47s, and was first shown to the public at the memorable Tinsley open day on 27 April 1996. The two locomotives, Nos 47807 and 47817, were to be seen on Virgin Cross Country services; shown here is No 47807, rounding the curve at Church Fenton at the head of the 07.55 Birmingham New Street-York on 3 May 1997.

No 47807 started as No D1639 on 14 December 1964 in green livery, becoming No 47055 on 18 May 1974, 47652 in July 1986 and 47807 on 10 July 1989. During these numerical changes it received firstly BR blue livery, and later large-logo blue (with West Highland Terrier motif between May 1987 and May 1988 while at Eastfield); InterCity colours appeared in July 1989, and the Porterbrook Leasing scheme in August 1996. It is currently in Virgin livery, which was applied at Crewe Works in March 1998.

heating of this area by flanging blocks), might result in a total tyre fracture. Therefore, a completely new type of 'narrow' block was designed, which was narrower in places and not susceptible to flanging. However, it reduced both the brake force available, as less of the block was in contact with the tyre, and block life; nor did it cure the problem, but merely contained it. Regional practices varied but, broadly speaking, this block was used as the gear wore and it was established that some or all of the brake blocks had started to 'flange'; as it could not be used selectively due to uneven wear rates, it had to be fitted in all positions. Generally, once it became necessary to use the narrow block, when repairs to the gear got beyond depot repair facilities, the owning depot would mark the outside of the locomotive 'narrow blocks only'. When blocking a 'foreign' locomotive, standing orders were to fit whatever type of block was already fitted, on the basis that the owning depot had fitted the correct type. This practice worked well; if it was not adopted, unscheduled repairs to brake gear became enormous. It must, however, be said that as the locomotives have ceased to be used on the high speed, high mileage work associated with the principal passenger services, brake gear wear and tear has been reduced. In addition, much work has been done over the years on hardening wearing surfaces, pins, bushes etc, to minimise wear.

Such has been the price of the leverage and linkage necessary to get two brake cylinders per bogie to operate 12 brake blocks!

At one stage in the mid-1970s, brake gear wear and tear on the fleet used on the East Coast main line (ECML) became so serious that a bogie overhaul became necessary, midway between Main Works 'classified' repairs; this was at an 18-month periodicity, against a then classified repair period of three years. It has to be remembered at this juncture that the Class 47/4s used on the ECML were covering the highest mileages of any locomotives in the fleet, around 100,000 miles per annum, at regular high speeds. It must also be pointed out that not all the brake gear wear and tear was necessarily due to actual use of the brakes. The design was such that a heavy slack-adjuster was mounted below the leading brake hangers

Above: The morning of 25 March 1989 was a bad day for diversions on the Settle & Carlisle as the first two trains had failures. No 47566, ex Springburn Works earlier in the month, failed on the 06.38 Glasgow-Euston, and had to be rescued by Railfreight No 47019. The train is seen approaching Garsdale.

No 47019 had led a nomadic existence around the system. When new as No D1573 in April 1964 it was one of the four originally allocated to Leeds Holbeck, where it remained for two years. It was then allocated to Gateshead, Haymarket, Immingham, Gateshead (again) and York, finally settling in October 1971 at Stratford, where it stayed for 14½ years. In May 1985 it was on the move again, to Cardiff Canton, and thence to Crewe, Bescot, Crewe (again), Tinsley and finally Old Oak Common in July 1991. It was eventually withdrawn on 24 January

1997 at Eastleigh. In spite of its movements between Regions and Sectors it only ran in BR green, BR blue and large-logo grey Railfreight liveries.

No 47566 also worked from many different depots. It started as No D1624 at Toton in October 1964. Frequent moves to the LM Western Lines and back to Toton occurred until September 1972 when it arrived at Tinsley. A six-year spell at Immingham began in May 1974, and was followed by a further six years at Stratford until the locomotive became redundant on the Great Eastern. Periods at Gateshead, Bristol and Crewe ensued until April 1991. It received TOPS No 47043 in February 1974, and became 47566 in May 1980. Livery changes saw it repainted into BR blue in May 1970, with silver roof added on 8 November 1980, and finally BR Main Line livery (as InterCity but with no logo) in March 1989.

Above: The main EWS depot at Toton has taken on major overhauls for Freightliner. Here No 47358 is seen receiving attention on 28 July 1997. It is in the two-tone grey livery introduced by Freightliner in 1995, which is now being superseded by the latest green livery. One of the non-boilered '47/3' sub-class, it entered service in June 1965 at Tinsley as No D1877.

Above: On Saturdays in May 1998, the train which had formed the 09.00 Poole-York returned as empty stock to Wolverhampton, and provided the only regular locomotive-hauled passenger stock working past Milford at this time. InterCity-liveried No 47841 The Institution of Mechanical Engineers is seen heading the Virgin coaches over the crossover.

This locomotive has had several identities, starting with D1726 at Landore on 18 March 1964. It remained allocated to the Western Region until May 1988, when it began a year in Scotland, at Eastfield depot. In the meantime it had been renumbered 47134 in March 1974 and 47622 in October 1984, eventually becoming No 47841 in December 1989.

Above: This 'Royal' engine began life as No D1656, entering traffic on 1 February 1965 allocated to Landore depot. Its first TOPS number was 47072, which it received on 29 January 1974. In April 1984 it became No 47609, in which guise it was named Fire Fly in a ceremony at Windsor & Eton on 24 August 1985, and then 47834 on 2 August 1989. Finally, when selected as one of the Royal locomotives, it was allocated No 47798, and renamed Prince William.

This loco spent the vast majority of its time on the Western Region, being allocated as follows:

2.65	Landore (new)
4.66	Cardiff Canton
8.67	Landore
10.70	Old Oak Common
5.75	Cardiff Canton
6.84	Old Oak Common
5.88	Bristol, Bath Road
5.89	Crewe
8.89	Bristol, Bath Road

It is now based at Crewe for its Royal duties, and operated by EWS.

Liveries carried have been:
BR green, when new
BR blue, from August 1969 (with silver buffers and larger numbers for naming, August 1985)
Early InterCity livery, from February 1987
InterCity 'Swallow' livery, from August 1989 (the first locomotive in this scheme)
Royal livery, from May 1995 (with body-side stripe added during 1997).
This picture was taken at Shipley on 14 May 1998, and shows the locomotive at the rear of the Royal Train taking HM The Queen from Hellifield to Bradford.

Left: No 47709 is featured elsewhere in the book in ScotRail livery. Here we see it in Fragonset colours, heading the 1M87 09.55 Penzance-Manchester express at Langston Rock on 20 September 1998. (Details of this locomotive's history and earlier liveries can be found on page 50.)

on all four corners of each bogie, and was liable to bounce about whilst the locomotive was running, causing all sorts of wear to the hanger, pull-rods and associated gear; clearly this was speed-related.

Locomotives were sent to Crewe Works every 18 months, where a completely overhauled set of bogies was substituted, and as locomotives were only sent when bogies were available, the actual time the locomotives were out of traffic was but a couple of days. However, the procedure was expensive and was not adopted by the other Regions operating the class, who managed to live with the narrow block alternative. The Eastern Region engineers considered this unacceptable in view of the work undertaken by the locomotives, and adopted the

Above: One of the most impressive InterCity trains was the 16-coach 'Orcadian' which ran regularly in the summer months from St Pancras to the Scottish Highlands. The picture shows that it included seven sleeping cars. No 47551 (sadly not as clean as the rest of the train) passes Holmes Junction, Rotherham on its way back to London on the evening of Monday 15 May 1989.

This locomotive has had many identities, starting with D1746 when allocated new to Old Oak Common. It became No 47153 under TOPS in May 1974, and then No 47551 in February 1975. In September 1989 it became No 47801, but reverted to 47551 in May 1992 as its long-range fuel tank was out of commission; since March 1993 it has been No 47774.

Its liveries have been less complicated. Delivered in BR green, in January 1972 it received BR blue, to which a silver roof was added in November 1984; a repaint into large-

logo blue followed in September 1986. The loco is currently running in Rail Express Systems red/grey colours, applied in March 1993. During its life it has been allocated all over the country, as follows:

7.64	Old Oak Common (new)
3.67	Cardiff Canton
10.67	LM Western Lines
6.68	Crewe
10.68	Toton
2.69	Crewe
12.69	Bescot
12.74	York
5.79	Laira
10.82	Old Oak Common
5.84	Stratford
5.85	Gateshead
1.87	Eastfield
5.88	Bristol, Bath Road
8.91	withdrawn
12.91	reinstated at Old Oak Common; (briefly withdrawn again 6.92 and reinstated)
7.92	Crewe.

Above: In the days before it became a 'celebrity' locomotive, No 47004 leaves Arbroath on the 12.36 Edinburgh-Aberdeen on 24 June 1989. Along with Nos 47152, 47206 and 47209 it was one of the last Class 47s in Scotland to have an operable boiler; this was isolated in October 1987, but still carried. Its last Works overhaul was completed on 18 January 1985. It was new as No D1524 in June 1963, and was allocated to the following depots:

6.63	Finsbury Park (new)
5.67	Tinsley
11.67	Finsbury Park
5.68	Tinsley
2.70	Stratford
10.71	York
4.72	Gateshead
5.72	Immingham
6.72	Stratford
9.73	Gateshead
5.75	Stratford
3.83	Eastfield
11.90	Tinsley
7.91	stored
7.91	withdrawn
11.91	stored
12.91	Old Oak Common
3.94	Stratford
12.95	stored
2.96	Toton [(briefly stored, 10.96)
9.97	Immingham
6.98	stored
6.98	Bescot
12.98	stored
12.98	withdrawn.

It was sent to Springs Branch for dismantling, but EWS then decided to send it to Old Oak Common for safe keeping, with the intention of exhibiting it at that depot's open day in the year 2000. We shall see the outcome in due course.

It carried few liveries, receiving BR blue in February 1971 (later embellished with a silver roof), which it retained until 1990. It then received two-tone grey, and was repainted BR green on 5 February 1994, when it was named Old Oak Common Traction and Rolling Stock Depot.

overhaul principle to obviate as far as possible the need for the narrow block.

As locomotive utilisation fell, upon the introduction of HSTs, brake wear was reduced, but by this time the periodicity between classified repairs had been extended to 9,900 engine hours, which roughly equated to five years. Thus the problem persisted, and in an effort to reduce costs, the Eastern Region instituted a procedure to continue the overhaul of brake gear at roughly midway between Works repairs. A spare set of Class 47 bogies was acquired, and the Regional Repair Shop at Stratford was equipped to change all the brake gear, and fit a service-exchange set, itself overhauled at Crewe. This ensured that a repaired set of bogies was available before the next locomotive was called in, and the actual time stopped was about the same as when Crewe did the work. Whilst the bogies were being overhauled the traction motors

1988, following the withdrawal of No 47406. By 1971 it was in BR blue, receiving large-logo blue in May 1987, Waterman Railways black in January 1995, and finally reverting to BR green in August 1998.

Above: On 18 October 1998 the West Coast main line electric services from Preston to Euston were diverted via Manchester, and were diesel-hauled as far as Crewe. The 09.50 Preston-Euston was hauled by Fragonset Class 47/4 No 47488, resplendent in the old British Railways green livery. It is shown near Manchester, Oxford Road, leading the DVT, with Class 90/0 No 90008 at the rear of the train.

The Class 47 entered service in BR green on 22 February 1964 as No D1713, receiving its TOPS identity in February 1974. It was named Rail Riders in May

Its allocations were:

2.64	LM Western Lines (new)
6.64	Cardiff Canton
7.65	Bristol, Bath Road
4.66	LM Western Lines
6.68	Bescot
11.85	Crewe
7.93	stored
10.93	withdrawn
12.94	reinstated at Crewe
2.95	withdrawn
3.95	reinstated to store
5.95	Cardiff Canton
7.96	stored serviceable at Crewe
9.97	to Fragonset.

Right: Unfortunately this smart livery was only applied to No 47972 in the Central Services pool. It was named The Royal Army Ordnance Corps in July 1989 when it appeared in the livery, and is seen on a test train at Paddington on 10 March 1994. On 12 November 1998 it was stored unserviceable at Crewe, and appears unlikely to run again.

The locomotive has had several identities since it was placed in service as No D1646 on 31 December 1964 at Cardiff Canton. It remained on the Western Region for just over 20 years before being allocated to Kingmoor,

Carlisle. It remained on the LMR Midland Division (except for six months at Bristol) until selected for the Central Services pool. It carried the following numbers: 47545, from November 1974; 97545, from September 1988; and 47972, from July 1989. It was originally allocated 47062 under TOPS, but never carried this.

Above: Diversions were in force on Sunday 19 December 1998 to avoid the Manchester Piccadilly area, and one of the trains rerouted was the 08.40 Glasgow-Penzance. Class 47/7 No 47702 was hauling the train, and is shown heading for Stockport on the single line section at Reddish South. It carries freshly-applied Virgin colours, having recently been hired to that company by EWS.

The locomotive was delivered from Brush in July 1966 as No D1947, being renumbered 47504 in March 1974, and 47702 in March 1979. Its allocations were as follows:

7.66	Toton (new)
10.66	LM Western Lines; then back to Toton
3.67	LM Western Lines; then LM Midland Lines
10.67	LM Western Lines
6.68	Bescot
11.69	Crewe
6.72	Bescot
11.72	Landore
2.73	Bristol, Bath Road
5.73	Landore
12.78	Haymarket
10.87	Eastfield
5.90	Old Oak Common
3.93	Eastleigh
7.93	Stratford
1.96	Toton
9.97	Immingham
10.98	Toton.

It has carried the following liveries:
BR green, from new
BR blue, from December 1972
ScotRail, from December 1984
Network SouthEast (revised version), from September 1990
Railfreight two-tone grey, from August 1994
Virgin red/grey, from September 1998.

Right: In addition to the Class 47s in this country, there were 10 locomotives built by Brush at Loughborough for Cuban National Railways in 1965. Due to the political situation between Dr Castro's Cuba and the USA, the locomotives were officially built by Clayton Equipment Co Ltd of Tutbury, and carried that company's works plates, although they were actually constructed at Loughborough. They were numbered 2501 to 2510 and painted in BR green, but were apparently repainted shortly after delivery.

Little is known about their working days in Cuba, but they probably suffered from a lack of spare parts. By February 1992, all but one of these locomotives were dumped at Cardinas, where this picture was taken, and had obviously not worked for some time. Two survivors were reported as recently as 1998.

were examined, and if the armature or field coils were below predetermined resistance levels, the opportunity was taken either to clean them, and thereby increase the internal resistance levels if this was possible, or replace them with overhauled units.

On the electrical side, there were all the normal problems encountered when new equipment is introduced, as staff got to know their way around the new machines, familiarising themselves with the schematics and wiring diagrams. Generally, much of the standard Brush type control equipment had already been proven in service, and was quite reliable. However, the type of interlock used on the various relays and contactors became a cause for concern, with its moving contacts habitually becoming detached from the main body of the block. A simple modification to retain the two halves together, by use of a plastic cover (easily detachable, and with a perspex front so that the operation of the interlock could be observed) cured the problem. This had the added advantage that

Above: Nos 47460 and 47461 were well-known Inverness locomotives during the 1980s. They are shown under repair inside the depot on 8 July 1989. Both locomotives started life at Gateshead in May 1964, following one another to Haymarket in October 1968 and then Immingham in October 1969. They then went their separate ways until being reunited at Inverness in October 1984.

No 47461 was named Charles Rennie Mackintosh at Glasgow Queen Street on 22 March 1982. After the initial green livery it received BR blue in June 1972. By May 1985 it had received the large-logo blue scheme, adorned with the 'Highland Stag' emblem, but in August was painted into the original InterCity livery. Change came quickly when it received the ScotRail logo and blue stripe in February 1986, for which it became well-known, being one of only two Class 47/4's to receive this treatment, No 47430 being the other. No 47461 had arrived on the Scottish Region in July 1979, and remained until ousted by Class 158s in October 1990, when it went to Crewe. It was stored on 1 January 1991 and withdrawn in April, being dumped in Basford Hall Yard.

No 47460 followed a similar pattern of allocation to 47461. It arrived at Haymarket in July 1979 and stayed at various Scottish depots until it was banished to Crewe in July 1991, where it remained until withdrawal on 6 January 1992. It had received the blue livery in January 1968, and had had a silver roof added at Stratford by March 1978; it gained the Inverness 'Highland Stag' emblem in March 1985, before receiving large-logo blue in October 1985.

it kept dirt from the contacts.

Yet another problem encountered by maintenance staff was with the 'Auto-Air' brake equipment fitted to later members of the class, starting with Loughborough-built No D1758 of May 1964. Although these problems were not directly related to the new locomotives, the Brush Type 4s were the first class of locomotive to have such equipment in any numbers, so obviously they bore the brunt of the learning curve. Once again, much concern was caused to members of the maintenance staff as they gained knowledge and became familiar with the new equipment. This applied to train crews too, and not a few problems were self-generated by drivers misusing the equipment, getting spurious symptoms, and making erroneous repair book entries. This could (and very often did) result in maintenance staff spending hours looking for faults that did not exist.

The brake system was made doubly complicated by a requirement for the locomotives to operate both air- and vacuum-braked trains. Although the system was air

Above: *The up 16-coach 'Orcadian' landcruise train has InterCity-liveried No 47824 Glorious Devon for motive power as it heads for St Pancras along the old Great Central route from Mexborough towards Rotherham, on 24 July 1989. This train headed north on the Friday, and returned on the Monday.*

The locomotive has had several identities, starting with D1780 when new in October 1964. It became No 47185 in November 1973, and 10 years later, in November 1983, No 47602. It was further renumbered as 47824 in April 1989, and finally adopted No 47782 on joining the RES fleet. It carried the Glorious Devon *name between August 1985 and February 1993. After green livery, it received BR blue, which it retained until July 1988, when it was* painted in the InterCity scheme illustrated. RES livery was applied in February 1994.

Its allocations have been:

10.64	Tinsley *(new)*
4.66	Stratford
5.71	Holbeck
3.73	Stratford
11.73	Bristol, Bath Road
7.74	Landore
7.74	Cardiff Canton
5.87	Old Oak Common
5.88	Crewe
4.89	Bristol, Bath Road
11.92	stored
2.93	Bristol, Bath Road
2.93	Crewe
5.93	Bristol, Bath Road
11.93	Crewe.

controlled, it was essential that, when a vacuum-braked train was being worked, the locomotive brake be proportional to the vacuum brake on the train. Hence, it was necessary for the locomotive to have equipment to convert the air 'message' from the driver's brake valve to a vacuum 'message' to operate the train brake, and then, in proportion to the vacuum brake applied to the train, convert this 'message' back again into air, so as to operate the locomotive's own straight air brake. This all contributed to an extremely complicated system, exacerbated by the need to accommodate four different braking rates, allowing for fitted, unfitted and partially fitted trains in both air and vacuum combinations,

as well as the emergency systems connected with the Automatic Warning System (AWS) and Driver's Safety Device (DSD).

We saw earlier how, in later batches of locomotives, early forms of electronic equipment were introduced. As was to be expected, this presented yet more difficulties for the maintenance staff, with a complete new philosophy to grapple with. Few depot electricians or supervisors were familiar with electronic equipment, and it was necessary to embark on an extensive series of training courses to equip staff at all levels with the requisite skills. It has to be added at this juncture that many very soon became extremely competent, and BR was able to take in its stride the rapid developments

Above: On 30 September 1989 No 47356 was just another Class 47/3 going about its normal duties in large-logo grey livery on an MGR working at Holywell on the North Wales main line.

Since then it has become the first member of the class to be converted into a Class 57 for Freightliner, fitted with a General Motors power unit.

The locomotive started its days at Immingham in July 1965 as No D1875, receiving its TOPS number in March 1974.

It then was allocated as follows:

10.65	Tinsley
3.70	Immingham
5.73	Crewe
5.75	Toton
11.78	Crewe
4.93	Bescot
5.95	Tinsley
3.96	stored
5.96	Tinsley
5.96	stored
12.96	Crewe
1.97	stored
2.97	Crewe
3.97	sent to Brush Traction at Loughborough, for conversion to Class 57.

Its liveries were BR green when new, BR blue from October 1977 and Railfreight large-logo grey from August 1986.

Above: No 47847 started as No D1774
when new in October 1964. Here it is
shown passing the site of the old Ardsley
steam depot on 18 February 1990 at the
head of empty Pullman stock which was
for a steam trip over the Settle-Carlisle line.
Allocations were as follows:

10.64	Darnall (new)
4.66	Stratford
5.71	Holbeck
10.72	Stratford
2.76	Holbeck
2.76	Knottingley
5.78	Healey Mills
5.80	Stratford
5.87	Eastfield
10.88	Crewe
5.92	Bristol, Bath Road
5.95	Crewe
3.98	Toton.

It received its original TOPS number,
47179, in July 1974, becoming
No 47577 March 1981 and finally 47847
in January 1990. It was named Benjamin
Gimbert GC between September 1981
and July 1987.

Its liveries were as follows:
BR green when new
BR blue, July 1974
BR blue with silver roof, May 1980
BR blue, March 1981
BR blue with silver roof, September
   1981
BR blue, February 1985
BR blue with silver roof, July 1985
Large-logo blue but retaining blue
   cabsides, January 1987
BR blue with silver roof, December 1989
InterCity 'Swallow' livery, 25 August 1990.

Some further explanation may be helpful
regarding this locomotive's livery variations.
   It was repainted by Stratford into that
depot's own version of large-logo blue,
which lacked the solid yellow cabsides. On
transfer to Eastfield it lost Stratford's
'Cockney Sparrow' emblem and gained
the 'West Highland Terrier'. Whilst at RFS,
Doncaster, for fitting of long-range fuel
tanks, no large digits were available and so
standard-sized ones were used, the
double-arrow symbol being erroneously
painted out at this time also, hence the
condition seen in this picture.

which were to follow in the field of electronic
equipment. The systems being discussed
here were, however, at a very early stage of
development, and it is amazing in retrospect
that they were as reliable as they were, and
that staff adapted to them so well. Initially, as
far as the depots were concerned, it was
merely a matter of component exchange, but
as familiarity grew, depots began to do more
and more repair work, renewing individual

printed circuit boards, and even on
occasions repairing them by fitting new
resistances, transistors and the like.

One other problem which deserves to be
highlighted at this point (and which leads
neatly into the next chapter) concerned the
steam heating equipment or, to use official
jargon, Carriage Warming Apparatus (CWA).
This single necessity, of using the new
traction with a large fleet of vehicles built to

be steam-heated, proved to be perhaps the single most troublesome factor in the whole dieselisation programme. It was quite common, in the railway press of the early and mid-1960s, to see pictures of passenger trains, diesel-hauled, but with a steam engine coupled inside for the sole purpose of providing train heat, due to failure of the equipment

Above: A regular duty for Immingham Petroleum sub-sector Class 47s in 1990 was the Glazebrook-Haverton Hill tanks. No 47380 with the later Petroleum emblem heads into Horbury cutting, just to the east of Healey Mills yard, on 5 March 1990.

This locomotive started as No D1899 in September 1965, receiving No 47380 in February 1974. It was named Immingham in September 1987, which it carried until withdrawal in July 1992, and was scrapped at Scunthorpe. The liveries carried were:

BR green, when new
BR blue, by June 1980
Railfreight 'red stripe', from July 1987
Railfreight Petroleum,
    from September 1988.

Allocations were as follows:

9.65	Immingham (new)
9.67	Tinsley
7.70	Immingham
10.73	Tinsley
5.74	Toton
6.74	Tinsley
2.77	Immingham
5.78	Tinsley
10.78	Immingham
5.79	Tinsley
9.79	Immingham
7.92	withdrawn.

Above: The Stourton-Crewe Freightliner passes Mirfield on 4 May 1990 headed by No 47451 in large-logo blue livery. It started life as No D1568 at Darnall in March 1964, finishing its career in May 1991 at Tinsley, only a mile or two away.

The locomotive received standard BR blue livery in December 1973, and large-logo blue in August 1986.

Its allocations were as follows:

3.64	Darnall (new)
4.64	Immingham
6.64	Finsbury Park
1.65	Immingham
4.65	March
5.68	Norwich
2.69	Tinsley
10.71	Immingham
7.73	Bescot
9.73	Crewe
7.90	Tinsley
7.90	stored
8.90	Tinsley
4.91	Tinsley
4.91	stored
6.91	withdrawn.

on the diesel. Despite the first 20 locomotives' being fitted with an additional dc generator to provide electric train heating, and an early decision that ac electric locomotives would also be equipped to provide an ETH supply, the remainder of the fleet was not so equipped. Although the coaches that the electric locomotives would haul over the West Coast main line (WCML) were converted for electric heating, there were no plans for a nationwide conversion programme. This may seem, and indeed with hindsight proved to be, a retrograde decision, but then as is often said, hindsight is an exact science . . .

Three types of equipment were fitted to the locomotives. The Stone-Vapor BR4625 steam generator was a development of earlier types, specially modified to a BR specification — hence the prefix — but still built under licence by Stone's of Deptford, based on the American Vapor patents. In this type of generator, often incorrectly described as a boiler, the water passes at very high pressure through the coils, and the oil fire surrounds them – sometimes they are referred to as 'water-tube boilers'. As the water gets hotter and hotter, and pressure increases, it 'flashes' into steam (hence the other oft'-used term, 'flash boiler'), and thereafter, for the remainder of its passage through the coils, its pressure and temperature increase. Such was the design that superheating, although not intended, was sometimes achieved! The equipment was designed to provide 'wet steam', at around 55psi, which was discharged down the train.

The Clayton steam generator worked on the same principle, the Mk II RO2500 (ie 2,500lb/hr capacity) being used, a development of the Mk I design and still built under licence from Clayton by English Electric at the Vulcan Foundry. This, like the Vapor design, broadly followed American thinking.

Both these steam generators were fully automatic, and as a consequence extremely complicated, presenting all manner of problems when mounted in a locomotive and subjected to a variety of riding conditions. Despite numerous modifications over a number of years, perfection was never reached, or even approached, and the

Clayton remained by far the more troublesome of the two. This piece of equipment was besieged by electrical problems, mainly on the control side, but there were also combustion problems, which generally resulted in a blocked coil unit. This had disastrous results, both for passengers and the environment, as clouds of black smoke would be emitted. Very often the coil units became so blocked before remedial action could be taken that it was impossible for depots to clean them in situ, and they had to be removed from the locomotive for repair, a time-consuming process.

By far the most simple, and as a result, the least troublesome, was the Spanner, a true fire-tube boiler, where the water surrounded the tubes, and the fire passed through them. This was of British design, and the Mk IIIB version found its way into the new locomotives. Unfortunately, the disadvantage of this boiler, which delayed its more general use, was its much lower steam output capacity — only 1,850lb/hr — and this limited the size of train it could adequately heat. The whole heating system was of the constant loss type, in that as the steam in the train condensed, it was discharged onto the 'four foot' via the traps which were mounted on the ends of each vehicle, as well as other places along the train.

Other problems connected with steam heating included freezing of the water supply in cold weather, and a steam coil was mounted in the 1,250gal underslung water tank, which could be fed with steam from the locomotive train pipe by opening a valve during freezing weather. Generally this would keep the water just above freezing point, unless the cold spell was particularly severe. However, the coils did have a tendency to rot away quite quickly, and between visits to Main Works, and were near-impossible to repair at depots without removing the tank, a difficult and lengthy job. Of course, when locomotives were stabled in freezing weather, precautions had to be taken, depending on how low the temperature dropped. Engines would be run for specified periods, as well as the boilers or generators, but sometimes several locomotives would be coupled together, and steam from one fed through to the others, so that each of the water tanks could be fed with steam without using the equipment on each locomotive.

Unlike some classes of locomotive there was no provision on these Type 4s for water pick-up from track water troughs, but the water tanks could be filled from platform-mounted steam engine water columns, through a circular aperture alongside the mid-body engine-room access door and thence via internal trunking. Most of these apertures have now been blanked off, and the internal trunking removed. I could say a lot more about steam-heating problems, but suffice to say, everybody was relieved when steam heating of passenger trains finally came to an end with the commencement of the 1986 summer timetable. The Scottish Region was the last to use steam heat, and as Class 37 locomotives were delivered after refurbishment with ETH fitted — the '37/4s' — the practice finally came to an end. When I arrived at Stratford in April 1985, there were still a few Class 47s with operative Spanner boilers, but the diagrammed requirement for them ceased the following month, with the introduction of the summer timetable. However, we continued to maintain them for a few more months, as a few excursion coaching stock sets that were steam-heated remained in service until the end of the summer.

Above: *In the summer of 1990, the afternoon Wilton to Felixstowe Freightliner called at Stourton terminal, Leeds, travelling from York via Castleford. No 47377 was in charge on the evening of 23 July, and the train is seen passing Monk Fryston, with Milford sidings in the background.*

The locomotive started life in September 1965 as No D1896, receiving its TOPS number in February 1974.

Its allocations have been as follows:

9.65	Tinsley (new)
10.68	Stratford
1.70	Immingham
10.73	Tinsley
11.73	Cardiff Canton
7.79	Bescot
7.84	Crewe
5.87	Cardiff Canton
5.88	Tinsley
10.95	Crewe.

The following liveries have been carried:

BR green, from new
BR blue, by August 1974
Railfreight Distribution (first livery), from April 1989
Railfreight Distribution (second livery), from September 1995
Freightliner, from January 1997.

5

Adapting to the Times

Following the decision to fit dual (air and vacuum) brake equipment on later Class 47 builds, it was further decided to fit the earlier members of the class, and this was accomplished as they passed through Crewe Works for general repairs. Apart from Nos D1500-19, which had Westinghouse brake equipment when new, the dual conversion equipment was of Davies & Metcalfe (D&M) type, but to ease the conversion of the first 20, a Westinghouse system was fitted, except for the compressors, which were of the standard D&M type, albeit powered by 800V (as opposed to 110V) motors.

The next significant modification stemmed from a decision to phase out steam-heating of passenger trains, as described in the last chapter. All locomotive-hauled rolling stock, commencing with the Mk 2a vehicles delivered from 1967, was either equipped for both systems (steam and ETH) or just ETH, and many of the earlier Mk 1 vehicles were converted to dual-heat. It was therefore essential that large numbers of diesel locomotives be equipped to provide a high-voltage supply, and almost overnight the first 20 locomotives, Nos D1500-19, came into their own. However, the question of how to equip the standard members of the class to provide ETH was not so easy, as provision with the same dc equipment fitted to the early locomotives would have been

Below: No 47593 Galloway Princess was a Scottish Region locomotive for almost 30 years. Having arrived with the 09.15 from Inverness, it is here seen leaving Elgin station to run round in the yard, where it waited prior to the 10.18 return working. It was new to Haymarket as No D1973 in November 1965, and was allocated around the Region. It became No 47272 under TOPS in September 1974, No 47593 in August 1983, and No 47673 in July 1991. On joining the RES fleet it was allocated No 47790.

It carried the following liveries:
BR green (from new)
BR standard blue by 1973, with silver roof added October 1979
Large-logo blue by July 1985

Original InterCity livery, from April 1994
RES livery, from December 1994.

Its depots allocations have been:

11.65	Haymarket (new)
10.65	Gateshead
10.69	Haymarket
8.83	Eastfield
3.91	Inverness
10.92	Btristol
5.93	Immingham
4.94	Crewe
11.97	Motherwell

Apparently it carried York InterCity Control nameplates in April 1994, although for how long is not known. It is currently back in the Scottish sleeper pool.

Above: The picture shows No 47901 on its final journey from Doncaster Works to MC Metals at Glasgow for scrapping. It was not fit to travel by rail so went by road, and is waiting for a police escort in the car park of the M62 motorway service station at Hartshead in West Yorkshire.

Its history is possibly the most interesting of any member of the class. It entered traffic as No D1628 at Toton in October 1964, and moved between Toton and Crewe depots until allocated to Immingham in June 1972, and then to Tinsley in October 1973. It returned to Immingham between October 1974 and January 1976 but was taken out of service due to an accident at Peterborough, after which it was sent to Crewe for repair. At this point the decision was taken to fit it with a 3,250hp Ruston-Paxman 16RK3CT engine plus other modifications which were going to be installed in the Romanian-built Class 56s. It emerged from Crewe in December 1975 and went to Tinsley for testing and to give

staff experience before the Class 56s arrived, staying until November 1979. The locomotive was re-engined again in 1979, this time with a Ruston-Paxman 12RK3ACT engine, initially rated at 3,300hp, to act as a test-bed for the forthcoming Class 58 design. It was then transferred to the Western Region, and although allocated to Cardiff and then Bristol it was always based at Westbury, where it worked stone traffic until withdrawn on 23 March 1990.

The locomotive was renumbered as 47046 on 24 November 1973, becoming 47601 on 4 January 1976, and finally 47901 in August 1979 to avoid its getting in the way of the '47/4' renumbering scheme. It was loaned to Toton during 1986 for comparison tests on pistons; it received further engine modifications when it visited Crewe Works in November 1988. It was green until November 1973, when it was painted blue, and kept this livery until receiving Railfreight Construction grey in March 1988.

enormously expensive, involving a complete new series of generators, and consequently main power unit bearers. Thus it was decided to adopt the system already used experimentally, and proving successful, on the last two locomotives delivered, Nos D1960/1.

The system on Nos D1960/1 utilised an auxiliary dual-wound alternator, itself replacing the auxiliary generator, mounted outboard of the main traction generator, and with sufficient capacity to provide locomotive auxiliary supplies at 110V, and some 400kW of train heating load. The overriding advantage of this system was a very modest increase in total locomotive weight, the space the equipment occupied inside the engine-room being not much more than the old auxiliary generator, a critical factor. There were two alternator three-phase output windings, and these used identical slots in the stator and were therefore magnetically coupled, so a common electronic voltage regulator managed both outputs. The use of an alternator, in saving both weight and space, also obviated the need for a commutator and associated brush gear, with reduced maintenance costs as a result. Both the ac outputs, auxiliary and ETH, were rectified by silicon diode full-wave bridge rectification. One winding provided auxiliary power at 110V nominal, and the other 825V nominal for the train heat supply. It was necessary to convert the ETH supply to dc, because the alternator provided polyphase variable-frequency current, due to engine speed changes. To ensure that the minimum ETH voltage was available at all times, provision was made marginally to increase the engine idling speed, and by insertion of a sleeve in the governor speed-setting piston, this was raised to 380rpm, resulting in the alternator running at 560rpm. In fact the ETH supply ranged between 775V and 920V, depending on auxiliary load, battery charge current and engine speed. Auxiliary and ETH rectifiers were both positioned in front of the alternator, so as to ensure that the diodes and their heatsinks were cooled by the air entering the alternator and generator. The additional control equipment associated with the modification was situated in cubicles above the rectifier bank and alternator.

There were slight differences between the equipment fitted to Nos D1960/1 and the later conversions, mainly as a result of service experience, but by and large they were the same. In the later conversions, after the phasing out of steam-heating, boilers were removed from the locomotives,

Above*: The days when No 47500 was one of the Western Region's prestige locomotives had long gone when this picture was taken of it hauling a diverted InterCity service between Leeds and Doncaster past Hunslet, Leeds, on 19 March 1992.*

It entered service as No D1943 on the West Coast main line in June 1966, was allocated TOPS number 47500 in March 1974, and in February 1979 was given the name Great Western, *which it carried until September 1991. The Western Region always kept it in excellent external condition, at first in BR blue and later in the Brunswick green applied for the GWR 150 celebrations in 1985. It received Rail Express Systems red/grey livery in November 1992 and was renumbered 47770.*

At the time of this picture it was allocated to Immingham and was frequently seen in

Leeds hauling Class 91s to Bradford, Forster Square, still in its green livery but without the nameplates and numberplates.

Its depot allocations were as follows:

6.66	LM Western Lines (new)
6.68	Bescot
9.68	Toton
3.69	Bescot
12.69	Crewe
5.72	Bescot
3.73	Landore
5.77	Bristol, Bath Road
11.77	Landore
3.78	Old Oak Common
5.88	Bristol, Bath Road
7.89	Crewe
7.91	Immingham
5.92	Crewe, joining the RES fleet 8.92

commencing with No 47556. These locomotives were also fitted with the next generation of electronic equipment, almost identical with that fitted to the High Speed Trains (HSTs), taking the form of printed circuits mounted on easily-removable trays, with separate trays for the various control functions. This was a far more compact layout, with all the electronic equipment grouped together, and resulted in a tremendous reduction in the time taken both in finding faults and in rectifying them after location, because complete function trays could be replaced in a matter of seconds. The opportunity was also taken to mount this equipment in the erstwhile boiler room, and this made the whole locomotive layout far better for access purposes, because although the equipment fitted neatly in the engine-room of the earlier conversions, it did make this area extremely cramped. The Eastern Region had the greatest requirement for dual-heat locomotives, because, while most of the night trains on the East Coast main line were steam-heated, all the daytime trains were electrically heated. This situation caused all sorts of operating

problems, and lasted until 1985, when Mk 3 sleeping cars arrived on the scene.

There were 135 locomotives authorised in the initial conversion programme, for the London Midland, Eastern and Western Regions, and under the TOPS renumbering scheme of 1974, these were placed in the range 47421-47555, following on from D1500-19 which had been renumbered 47401-20. The electronic load regulators fitted originally were of Brush type ACR1, and operated on the separate field of the main generator, working in conjunction with a positive transducer, which was located on, and driven by, the engine governor servo-motor. Series-parallel conversions were renumbered as 47401-54, with all parallel conversions numbered upwards from 47455; all later conversions were of the latter variety, the '47/4' number series eventually reaching 47665. Subsequently, authority was given to convert more locomotives until a total of 264 was fitted, including those locomotives further converted to Class 47/7, and the programme was completed by 1986. The '47/7s' were additionally fitted with equipment for push-pull operation, whereby a locomotive can be remotely driven from a driving cab in a coach at the opposite end of the train. These locomotives were for the Scottish Region, initially to operate the Glasgow-Edinburgh half-hourly service, but later additional locomotives were converted, to embrace a number of Glasgow/ Edinburgh-Aberdeen dia-grams too. The push-pull

Above: InterCity-liveried No 47818 is shown, minus Swallow emblem, passing through the southern suburbs of Leeds at Hunslet, at the head of the diverted 14.43 York-Plymouth on 18 April 1992. Its first allocation was to Cardiff Canton in December 1965 as No D1917, and then as follows:

10.86 Gateshead
5.87 Eastfield
5.88 Bristol, Bath Road
9.91 Crewe
11.91 Bristol, Bath Road
5.95 Crewe
3.98 Toton.

The liveries carried have been:
BR green, from new
BR blue, from November 1973
InterCity (Mainline), from February 1989 (as illustrated)
InterCity (Swallow), from May 1993
Virgin red/grey, from January 1999.

equipment used Railway Clearing House (RCH) train lighting jumper cables, which connect between the coaches; by sending predetermined messages at differing voltages, the equipment on the locomotive senses the voltage, interprets the message, and operates the controls accordingly.

By 1974 the average life of the fleet was some 10 years, out of an originally-envisaged 'book' life of 20 years, and it was becoming obvious that unless something quite drastic was done, many of them would become completely uneconomic to maintain; paradoxically it was becoming equally apparent by this time that many would be required to last longer than 20 years. Among the items causing concern were the power units, and we have already seen the major problems they had caused in the early days. Because of the constant need for depots to take cylinder heads on and off, due to an inability to find a successful method of keeping them watertight, much wear and tear of the heads themselves and the top land (surface) of the cylinder block had taken place. Similarly the top and bottom water seals on the cylinder liners had never been fully successful, despite many modifications in the way they were sealed, and like the heads, constant removal and replacement had badly worn the cylinder block mating surfaces. Not least, many of the crankcases, where the bearing saddle alignment was in danger of exceeding tolerance, would need reboring.

Thus a scheme for a mid-life refurbishment was evolved, which became known as the Heavy General Repair programme (HGR), and work started at Crewe in 1976. At a planned rate of two locomotives per week, it was reckoned to complete the whole fleet in five years. In actual fact it took a little longer, and was often accompanied by conversion to ETH. The specification was designed around many of the features I have already outlined, as well as all number of smaller improvements in areas where experience had dictated there were serious problems affecting reliability and availability. With the exception of their very early years, the locomotives had never been able to sustain the original projected 90% availability, having struggled to get near 80%, and the ETH conversions rarely attained much more

than 70%; likewise miles-per-casualty only rarely exceeded 25,000. The opportunity was also taken to remove boilers (where this could be done) and boiler water tanks (strengthening the battery box support arrangement in the process), and to carry out any other previously authorised modifications. Another problem that arose as locomotives approached 10 years old was of severe fractures developing in the body underframe cross-stretchers, where the bogie pivot was mounted on the underside of the main frame; some redesign encompassing complete replacement of the cross-stretchers improved the arrangement. Another aspect of the programme entailed rewinding many of the traction motors, and the addition of many completely new motors to the total pool.

Replacement cylinder heads were fitted, to a new design, and embodying many improvements, not least in the area of the core plugs, where much fracturing had taken place over the years. The new design improved the stress areas, and general coolant distribution. Just as this work got underway, the locomotives suffered from a spate of valve stem fractures and valve insert failures, variously attributed to a defective material specification and incorrect heat treatment of the valves. As a rule it was the exhaust valves that failed, usually towards the drive end of the engine, because temperature got much higher there.

The opportunity was taken to remove much other redundant equipment during the repair, including route indicators, air refuelling equipment and several other odd items. There was some tidying up and selective renewal of the wiring and, in the case of the first 20, some quite major electrical alterations. These locomotives had suffered all their lives from having the 110V auxiliary and 800V ETH circuits sharing the same trunking and junction boxes. What ought to have been quite minor repairs after ETH wiring faults resulted in major rewiring of the control circuitry, after burning of the high voltage cables had also caused damage to the low voltage ones. Many of these locomotives had had to go to Main Works for repairs, so extensive was the wiring damage. There were also problems

Above: Well away from Network SouthEast territory, on 21 May 1992 No 47587 is seen arriving at Bolton with parcel vans from Crewe, as Class 08 No 08694 waits to shunt the stock. Note where the nameplate used to be, removed when the locomotive was reallocated to Crewe. It had carried the name Ruskin College Oxford between October 1990 and May 1992 when it was usually employed on Paddington-Oxford services.

Numbered D1963 when it entered service in September 1965, the Class 47 became No 47263 under TOPS in February 1974, No 47587 on ETH conversion in March 1983 and finally No 47736 in the RES fleet, being renamed Cambridge Traction and Rolling Stock Depot.

Its allocations were as follows:

9.65	Cardiff Canton (new)
1.66	Crewe
4.66	LM Western Lines
6.68	Crewe
1.73	Immingham
10.73	Gateshead
3.74	Immingham
1.81	Finsbury Park
2.81	Stratford
5.82	Immingham
3.83	Stratford
5.86	Gateshead
10.87	Inverness
5.88	Old Oak Common
10.88	Laira
5.89	Old Oak Common
5.92	Crewe.

The following liveries were carried:
BR green when new
BR standard blue by July 1973
BR blue with silver roof, from February 1982
BR standard blue, from June 1983
BR blue with silver roof, from September 1985
Large-logo blue with silver roof, from May 1988
Network SouthEast (revised), from October 1990
RES red/grey, from October 1993.

with the location of the body-side junction boxes, water managing to penetrate them as they abutted the engine-room roof/body interface. Indeed, there was a time when, despite our efforts at sealing these boxes, we were sure to get at least one locomotive with electrical problems as a result of water ingress after long periods of wet weather, often with the disastrous results described above. Thus a lot of work went into separating the two circuits, 110V and 800V, and redesigning the junction boxes to ensure they were watertight. At this time most of these locomotives were still at Finsbury Park, and engaged on some of the hardest and longest diagrams operated by the class, very often turn and turn about with the 'Deltics'. Several members of the depot staff were able to visit Crewe Works and help in the redesign work from a practical point of view as the locomotives were actually being modified; they were thus able to observe the progress of work on a series of locomotives that had been allocated to their depot since new.

6

Cost-Effective Maintenance

In the early 1980s, it was becoming increasingly obvious that, if BR was to make the advances in cost-effectiveness that were essential for its survival, a complete rethink of its approach to traction and rolling stock maintenance was necessary. An in-depth study was therefore commissioned, using both in-house and external sources. By and large, the repair philosophy for traction and rolling stock in this country had altered but little from steam days in that, when various components became so worn that depot rectification was difficult if not impossible, a locomotive would be taken to a Main Works, and given a 'General' overhaul. By definition, this would result in many components being repaired before they needed such attention, and when they were midway through their respective 'ideal' repair cycles. However, in a 'cut your losses' type environment, this had been the procedure adopted since time immemorial, to enable locomotives to run with minimum attention until their next general repair dates. The Class 47s were scheduled to visit Crewe Works for repair at intervals of between three and five and a half years. The actual periodicity for individual locomotives was based on 9,900 engine hours, and this averaged three and three-quarter years for a Class 47/7, five years for a Class 47/4, and

Above: On unusual work for a Railfreight Distribution locomotive, due to the non-availability of a Class 37/4, No 47249 prepares to leave Salford Crescent with the 07.16 Southport-Manchester on 26 June 1992. It is in the smart 'red stripe' Railfreight livery, and has painted on the side the unofficial name 'Sea Hawk', which was applied at Tinsley on 15 November 1991.

As No D1926 this locomotive entered traffic at Cardiff Canton in December 1965, but during the latter part of 1966 it moved to Eastleigh with others to help out the ailing Bulleid Pacifics. After this it moved frequently between the LMR and WR, eventually settling at Bristol Bath Road for nine years between 1978 and October 1987, when it joined the Railfreight Distribution fleet at Tinsley. Its last working was in August 1994, after which it was stored unserviceable. One of its cabs was later used to repair collision damaged No 47200. On 2 March 1998 it was moved from Tinsley to Booth's at Rotherham, where it was cut up.

New in BR green, it was in BR blue by April 1973, and received the Railfreight 'red stripe' livery in June 1987.

Above: On 5 September 1992 No 47823 leaves Bradford Forster Square with empty stock, heading for Keighley to collect passengers for a trip over the Settle-Carlisle railway.

This locomotive began life as No D1757 in September 1964, and has carried several numbers. Having forsaken green for BR blue, in February 1974 it received the number 47163, and in 1977 was one of the locomotives to have the Union Jack applied by Stratford depot for HM The Queen's Silver Jubilee celebrations. Adopting No 47610 in April 1984, it became 47823 in April 1989, and finally, on joining the RES fleet, it was given No 47787.

It has been allocated as follows:

9.64	Cardiff Canton (new)
1.67	Landore
7.68	Crewe
1.69	Bristol, Bath Road
3.69	Stratford
10.80	York
3.81	Tinsley
6.81	Haymarket
10.82	Eastfield
7.84	Inverness, then Eastfield
5.85	Crewe
5.86	Bescot
11.86	Crewe
4.89	Bristol, Bath Road
3.94	Crewe.

Liveries carried have been:
BR green, from new
BR blue, from December 1969
BR blue with Union Jack, from June 1977
BR (standard) blue, from June 1979
BR blue with silver roof, from September 1979
BR (standard) blue, from September 1984
InterCity (Mainline), from September 1988
InterCity (Swallow), from June 1991
RES red/grey , from December 1994.

five and a half years for a Class 47/0.

The Achilles heel for steam locomotives, ie the components that determined the 'shopping' periodicity, was generally boilers and axleboxes; with diesels it was bogies and power units, in particular in the former case tyre life and brake gear wear and tear. One conclusion drawn from the study was that the time had come to discontinue the practice of general repairs and move towards life-expiring individual components, but at the same time ensuring reliability did not suffer.

This philosophy was aided by a general move, in the newer types of traction and rolling stock, towards designing for component exchange, with the use of modular replacement for many groups of equipment. This, of course, had to result in far better machinery and equipment layouts in the locomotives, enabling depots to change equipment far more easily. There was also much less need, in many cases, to dismantle almost entire locomotives, to gain access to one particular item!

To take the enormous fundamental step of reducing the need for Main Works overhauls, it was essential to consider almost all types of locomotives, old and new. That is, all classes that had any sort of future under the new rules, and with over 500 members still in service, and large numbers of them needed for at least another 10 years, the Class 47s had to be a part of the new philosophy. As we have already seen, despite these locomotives' being to some extent a second-generation diesel design, they were somewhat hastily conceived, before the lessons of the first generation were properly understood and evaluated, and so bore heavily on their predecessors. Therefore, little thought had

been given during the design towards component exchange, in the context of Cost-Effective Maintenance. Nevertheless, to make the New Maintenance Policy (NMP) work, the Class 47s had to be included, by sheer weight of numbers, if by no other criterion.

Thus, in an attempt to see exactly what was involved, a decision was taken to undertake what amounted to a Main Works repair on a Class 47 locomotive in a regional workshop. There were several reasons for this: in the first place it was necessary to see just what was involved with a Class 47, in view of the factors outlined in the previous paragraph; in the second, so far removed had BR and its subsidiary BREL become since the

Below: Hertfordshire Railtour duties for Postal-liveried No 47501 *Craftsman*, passing the long-closed station at Leyburn on the Wensleydale line on 20 September 1992.
   The locomotive has had only two numbers: D1944 when new in July 1966, and 47501 which it received in February 1974. Its liveries were as follows:
BR green, when new
BR blue, by 1973
Large-logo blue, from June 1986
InterCity (original livery), from January 1987
Parcels, from August 1990.

The depot allocations were:

7.66	LM Western Lines (new)
6.68	Bescot
12.69	Crewe
6.72	Bescot
10.76	Crewe
12.79	Laira
1.80	Landore
10.82	Old Oak Common
3.88	Bristol, Bath Road
11.91	Crewe
11.96	stored
11.96	Crewe
10.97	stored
12.97	Crewe
3.99	withdrawn

(last working 5Z39 King's Cross-Bounds Green ecs).

latter became a separate company in 1968, that nobody on the Regions really knew what was involved in classified repairs, or what was the general condition of many of the components removed for overhaul. There was only one regional depot with anything like the facilities traditionally on hand in a Main Works, and this was the Traction Repair Shop (TRS) at Stratford, in East London. This shop had been the 'new' erecting shop of Stratford Works, when Stratford was a Main Works itself, prior to its closure as such in 1963. Retained then by the Eastern Region as a repair shop to relieve its depots of some of their larger and heavier work on diesel locomotives, it had since undertaken all sorts of other tasks. Of the three bays, the outer ones were traversed by twin 40-ton Electric Overhead Travelling Cranes (EOTC), which were capable of lifting not just locomotive power units, but complete locomotive bodies too; moreover, such was their design that they could be enhanced, at little cost, to lift 50 tons each.

A lot of preliminary work was undertaken in analysing the existing Main Works repair schedule, and deciding what was and was not to be done, and how the job should be tackled. Spring came and went, and summer marched on, before agreement was eventually reached to 'stop' locomotive No 47007, due a classified repair at Crewe, and undertake the work at Stratford. In fact, although it was the intention to undertake a full repair, except on a few items where this had already been deemed unnecessary, Stratford would not, of course, repair all the various components removed, but instead exchange them for previously overhauled ones from Crewe Works. Thus was born the term Component-Exchange Maintenance (CEM).

Locomotive No 47007 was not the first choice, but fell into the category of not being ETH-fitted, having series-parallel connected traction motors, no known serious defects, and being due a general repair in the 1986/7

Above: Against the background of the fine Midland Railway station buildings at Shipley near Bradford, Railfreight Distribution's No 47052 arrives on 18 March 1993 with empty wagons for scrap to be collected from Crossley's yard.

Entering traffic as No D1634 on 14 November 1964, it started life at Crewe, before moving to the Western Region until June 1968. It then had 10 moves around the London Midland Region, before being allocated to Holbeck in October 1974. It only stayed there for two months before making another 10 moves around the Eastern/North Eastern Regions, eventually settling at Tinsley with Railfreight Distribution.

After its original green livery, it received BR blue in December 1975 (with silver roof added by November 1984), and the initial Railfreight Distribution livery in November 1988. It received Freightliner livery in October 1996

programme. Picking a non-ETH locomotive was deliberate, and on two counts; it was desirable neither to over-complicate the job, when so little experience was on hand, nor (as the repair would probably take some time to complete) to reduce the number of available ETH locomotives, which were still at a premium at that time.

The locomotive was 'stopped' on 12 September 1986, and an organised strip-down commenced, Stratford fitters removing all the components and in some instances — the fuel tanks are a case in point — wondering why they needed to be removed at all, when there appeared to be nothing wrong with them. As with the fuel tanks, each item removed was studied and analysed by representatives from the Depot, Freight Engineer and the Specialist Engineers, deciding in each case what any future repair policy should be. Frequent meetings were held, usually on site at Stratford, to collate the results, thoughts and ideas, and gradually a new schedule emerged. It was also decided to adopt a 'depot', rather than 'Works', nomenclature, and the new exam was christened an 'F' examination, continuing the existing 'A' – 'E' sequence, the 9,900 engine hours periodicity being maintained. By this time, this averaged three and three-quarter years for a Class 47/7, four and a half to five and a half years for a Class 47/4, and four and a half to six years for a Class 47/0.

As well as checking the actual examination items, the opportunity was taken to consider any modifications that might be required, as

contemporary practice was to make these when locomotives visited Main Works for classified repairs. Again, analysis of modifications made to No 47007 enabled decisions to be made on which should be pursued, bearing in mind their usefulness, cost, and the expected life of the locomotives. By definition, this identified those which should not be continued. It has to be said that most were abandoned!

When the time came to put the patient back together again, Stratford really began to learn lessons! Few, if any, jobs on No 47007 had not been done before at Stratford, but never all at the same time; all sorts of problems arose in putting all the removed components back again, particularly in the brake compartment, where a lot of individual valves etc had been disturbed, not to mention their connecting pipes and reservoirs. However, this helped solve a question over the level of attention to be given to individual brake components at the 'F' examination. Experience had shown that few of the valves lasted between scheduled overhauls without some form of attention, and it was felt there was little point in disturbing a working valve at the 'F' examination, if the depot would have to give it attention later anyway. The resulting exclusion of these items had tremendous advantages in reducing the time taken commissioning repaired locomotives. Brake faults are amongst the most difficult to trace, so complicated is the equipment on dual-

Above: *Using a departmental train as a means of moving locomotives south from Carlisle, No 47308 in Railfreight grey livery heads Class 31/1 No 31304 and Class 37/7 No 37714 on 14 May 1994. The cavalcade is rounding the curve at Low Gill on the West Coast main line.*

The Class 47 was new in December 1964 as No D1789, adopting its TOPS identity of 47308 in November 1973.

Its depot allocations have been:

12.64	Tinsley (new)
3.69	Thornaby
10.71	Knottingley
8.79	Healey Mills
9.84	Thornaby
1.87	Tinsley
6.92	stored
9.92	Tinsley
7.93	stored
1.94	Tinsley
3.94	Bescot
8.95	stored
3.98	Crewe.

Liveries have been as follows:
BR green, when new
BR blue, from November 1973
Railfreight two-tone grey, from April 1988
Departmental ('Dutch' grey/yellow), from
    July 1994
Freightliner, from June 1998.

In 1998 it had multiple-working equipment fitted, but not long-range fuel tanks.

braked locomotives, and can be far more easily located when the extent of disturbance during repair has been limited.

Shortly before work commenced, the BRB's New Maintenance Policy was announced, and this coincided with a round of depot rationalisations which removed what had been a long standing question mark over Stratford Repair Shop's future. As the TRS had been given renewed life, it was decided that locomotive No 47007 should be named *Stratford*, on conclusion of its repair. The ceremony itself was timed to take place before contractors arrived to make alterations to the depot, to enable it to undertake the new 'F', 'G' and 'H' examinations on diesel and electric locomotives. On Saturday 15 November 1986, there gathered together at Stratford a large number of Stratfordians, past and present, together with their wives,

families and friends along with a number of invited guests, to witness T. C. B. (Terry) Miller Esq, a former Stratfordian himself, unveiling the nameplates. Terry Miller had been in charge of the Stratford Motive Power District for 10 years from 1947, and when CME of the Eastern Region was instrumental in the 1963 decision to retain the shop when the Works closed, so a no more fitting person could have been considered. With him and his wife on the rostrum, were Mr L. T. T. (Theo) Steel, Assistant General Manager, Eastern Region and myself, along with our wives. It was indeed a memorable day, and a good time was had by all, this being the culmination of an absorbing few months for all of us at Stratford. Locomotive No 47007 thereafter returned to normal service, none the worse for its experience, and (those of us at Stratford at the time would claim) a good deal

better than before its participation in the events just described; indeed, it can truly be said that a lot of people learned a lot about locomotives, resulting from their experiences with No 47007!

The locomotive was not actually released until 9 December 1986, as it had to go to Tinsley for load bank testing, there being at that time no such facility at

Above: The morning of 28 May 1994 was fine and sunny around Sheffield, as No 47843 headed north past Kilnhurst with the 07.55 Birmingham-York, the train travelling via Leeds.

The locomotive was new to Cardiff Canton in April 1965 as one of the Western Region's named locomotives, No D1676 Vulcan. Except for a two-year spell at Stratford in 1969/70, it put in 24 years' service on the Western Region, moving

frequently between the main depots. On 14 May 1989 it went to Crewe to join the InterCity fleet, and is currently still clocking up the miles on Virgin Cross Country services. It has carried the numbers 47090 (from March 1974), 47623 (from November 1984), and finally 47843 (from March 1990). It received blue livery by February 1973, which it retained until March 1990 when it received the InterCity Swallow livery shown here.

Stratford. Load bank testing is necessary to adjust an individual locomotive's separate field ballast resistors against individual generator character-istics, when power units are changed. Usually only minor adjustments are needed (if any) but failure to make them can affect the ability of the generator to follow its designed power curve. This can result in either under- or over-powering, and

Above: Rail Express Systems-liveried Class 90/0 No 90016 required the assistance of similarly-painted Class 47 No 47778 Irresistible on the Low Fell-King's Cross parcels, seen passing Burn on the East Coast main line on 17 March 1995.

The Class 47 has had many identities over the years since it entered service in March 1965 as one of the Western Region's named locomotives, No D1666 Odin. On 23 February 1974 it became No 47081, then No 47606 on 21 February 1984, and No 47842 in February 1990, reverting to

47606 in February 1993. Finally it joined the RES fleet as No 47778 in March 1993. Its original name was carried until July 1990, although the plates were removed for short periods.

By 1974 it had gained BR blue livery; the early InterCity livery was applied in October 1987, and replaced by the 'Swallow' version in February 1990. It received its RES colours in March 1993. Up until 16 May 1988, when it was reallocated to Crewe, it had spent its entire life on the Western Region.

the possibility of generator overload, with disastrous results, cannot be ruled out. It is also useful to check all the connections etc, and make any necessary adjustments to the crankcase depression under simulated full load conditions.

Following the overhaul of No 47007, a working party was formed, consisting of representatives from all the depots which were going to undertake the new 'F' exams on Class 47s (ie Stratford, Doncaster, Springburn and BREL Crewe), along with staff from the Freight Engineer and the Specialist Engineers at the Railway Technical Centre in Derby. The group was chaired by Jim Vine, Project Manager, New Maintenance Policy, and under his able leadership much was achieved. We met regularly, to review experience gained on No 47007, ensure all the depots knew what was expected of them, and generally discuss training, the supply of equipment, material and all sorts of other issues.

An early decision was taken to undertake a further 'pilot' exercise, before the full introduction of NMP, by then planned for 1 April 1987 and again, in view of its achievements and facilities, Stratford was chosen for the work. This time it was decided to repair an ETH-fitted locomotive to gain experience of this sub-class, and as Stratford-based No 47581 was due a classified repair before the end of the 1986/7 financial year, this locomotive was selected. It was of course a very apt choice anyway, carrying as it did the name *Great Eastern*, and work commenced on 12 February 1987. As was to be expected, this turned out to be a much simpler exercise than on No 47007, being straightforward in most respects. Stratford was able to draw on experience previously gained to complete an 'F' examination to a refined schedule; in so doing, additional minor lessons were learned, leading to further revisions in specifications. No 47581 was released in early April, as the new procedures were coming on stream.

From 1 April 1987 the whole class was subject to NMP, undergoing 'F' examinations

---

Below: The power was switched off between Neville Hill depot at Leeds and the City station on Sunday 30 April 1995, so Class 91s required dragging. No 47703 Lewis Carroll, *ex works in the smart Waterman Railways black livery, was employed on this duty. It was new as No D1960 for duties on the West Coast main line in July 1967 and was then allocated as follows:*

6.68	Crewe
4.71	Toton
2.72	Crewe
2.73	Toton
12.78	Haymarket
10.87	Eastfield
11.90	Crewe
7.91	Old Oak Common
2.93	Eastleigh
7.93	Crewe
8.97	Tyseley.

Liveries have been:
BR blue with double-arrow symbol at both ends, from new
Standard BR blue, September 1975
BR blue with silver roof, November 1979
ScotRail, May 1985
Parcels Sector red, January 1991
Waterman Railways black, April 1995
Fragonset Railways, January 1998.

Above: The Crewe Works test train (5D06) was a familiar sight along the North Wales coast, working at one time to Holyhead. Two RES Class 47s are seen approaching Penmaenmawr on 22 June 1995.

Heading the train is No 47760 *Restless.* This locomotive has been allocated widely over the system, starting with Toton when new in August 1964 as No D1617. It remained on the London Midland Region at various depots until going to Tinsley via Stratford depot in December 1972. May 1974 saw it at Immingham, where it stayed until transferred to Eastfield in May 1977. It remained at Scottish depots until 18 November 1992, when it returned to the LMR at Crewe. It had several numbers: 47036 from 23 March 1974; 47562 from

1 November 1979; and 47672 from 9 July 1991 until January 1993, when it reverted to 47562. More recently it has become No 47760. On 19 September 1983 at Glasgow Queen Street it was named Sir William Burrell by Princess Anne. It had lost BR green for BR blue by March 1969, small 'West Highland Terrier' emblem being added in April 1986; Mainline colours were applied in June 1989, and RES by September 1991.

Behind is No 47625 *Resplendent,* before it became No 47749 *Atlantic College* on 17 November 1995. The locomotive has had several identities since it was new to Landore in February 1965, when it was named *City of Truro* and numbered D1660. It remained on the Western Region until 1988, moving between the main depots. It became No 47076 in February 1974 and then No 47625 in November 1984. Repainted from green to blue in 1971, it at first lacked the BR double-arrow symbol, acquiring this in August 1973. Mainline livery appeared in January 1989, and finally RES livery in 1991.

at 9,900 engine-hour intervals at the depots previously outlined, with British Rail Engineering Ltd (BREL) at Crewe, undertaking its quota on a contractual basis. However, 1986 had seen the first large inroads into the class, significant numbers being withdrawn as the rail business was further rationalised, and the locomotive fleets sectorised and sub-sectorised. A 'hit list' was established of locomotives with series-parallel-connected traction motors, which were nearing their erstwhile classified repair dates; any serious defect would result in their withdrawal. Additionally, the opportunity was taken to withdraw, rather than repair, any locomotive seriously damaged in a collision or derailment. The decision to select the series-parallel locomotives was a result of there being fewer of them, and of their general lower reliability and greater maintenance costs, the latter largely due to a higher incidence of traction motor flashovers.

It also allowed the spares float of certain critical major spares, ie wheel sets, power units and some of the auxiliary machines to be enhanced. Furthermore, these locomotives were the oldest in the fleet, first to have undergone HGRs, and becoming due for their next general repair. As more locations would be undertaking the new 'F' examinations than were ever involved in the former classified repairs, increased floats of the components to be changed were essential to cover the movement of parts between depot and repairer. Consequently, there was a need either to withdraw some members of the class to provide more spares or to order additional spares, and as some members of the class were becoming surplus, the former was the logical answer. Several withdrawn locomotives were deposited at the depots that were going to undertake the work, to enable parts to be removed and put into the spares float.

The first year's experience of NMP was extremely successful, over 80 locomotives being involved, each depot undertaking the work achieving its output targets, and by and large within previously stipulated down-times. The fleet continued to perform as well as previously, and indeed, there were small increases in availability as the new examinations necessitated the locomotives' being out of traffic for a shorter time than did the old Works repairs — one of the objectives of NMP. Neither were there any consequent reductions in reliability, which in part compensated for the locomotives withdrawn to provide spares.

For the second year of the programme, the financial year 1988/9, fewer locomotives (74) needed 'F' examinations, due to an increasing withdrawal rate, and thus the work was concentrated on the BR depots of Doncaster, Springburn and Stratford, with results showing a similar success rate to the first year's. Of course, whilst all this work was going on, every opportunity was taken to refine the schedule of work to be undertaken, in the light of experience, and many items were either removed altogether, or rescheduled for one of the depot examinations. In the odd case, experience demonstrated a need not only to replace items previously deleted, but also to

Above: Another picture of the Crewe test train, taken at the same spot as the previous photograph. No 47519, freshly repainted in BR green, is seen piloting No 47640 University of Strathclyde, on 28 June 1995.

As No D1102, No 47519 was one of a batch of 12 allocated new to York in October 1966 for East Coast main line duties. It was not until 5 October 1980 that it was transferred, to Stratford.

Its subsequent allocations were:

2.81	Immingham
10.82	Gateshead
4.86	Inverness
5.87	Eastfield
11.87	Old Oak Common
5.88	Bristol, Bath Road
4.89	Crewe
7.91	Immingham
4.92	Crewe
11.96	stored
11.96	Crewe
4.97	Toton
9.97	Immingham
11.98	Bescot
3.99	stored unserviceable.

Its liveries were:
BR green when new
BR blue, summer 1973
BR blue with silver roof, December 1980
BR blue, July 1982
Large-logo blue, April 1986
BR green, June 1995.

It received its TOPS number in February 1974. As part of a minor overhaul in 1995, it was fitted with long-range fuel tanks and repainted BR green for charter work, which it only did on a very few occasions. It was then transferred to Railfreight Distribution.

No 47640 was new as No D1921 in January 1966 and spent some time on the Southern Region to help out at the end of steam services. It received its original TOPS number, 47244, in May 1974 and became 47640 in February 1986. After BR blue livery, it received the large-logo style in 1986, and Parcels Sector red in 1991. It was named University of Strathclyde in April 1986, which it still carried in April 1999. Its days must be numbered and it may be history by the time this book appears.

reschedule items to the 'F' examination from the 'A' – 'E' sequence; indeed, despite almost 30 years' experience with the locomotives, the odd completely new item had to be added. The year 1989/90 required 69 locomotives to receive an 'F' examination, the work being split between Doncaster and Stratford.

All in all, NMP proved to be extremely successful, not only in terms of massive cost reductions, but in improvements in availability, with no loss of reliability. BREL Crewe remained the main contractor for component repairs, with the depots forecasting their requirements months in advance, based on their programmed workload, and refining these a week or so before each locomotive was due to be 'shopped'. This way, the depots' Materials Managers and their suppliers could gear up to ensure that the necessary parts were to hand just when they were needed. So, despite early concern expressed by many who were familiar with the Class 47s when the policy was first announced, these locomotives were transferred to a completely new maintenance philosophy, for which they were not designed, with enormous success. That this should take place in their twilight years was not only interesting from an engineering point of view, but a sound lesson in what can be achieved, and a vindication of those who had the foresight to drive the policy forward. That I was so closely involved in this during my tenure at Stratford gives me no small pleasure, and made the four years I spent there among the most enjoyable and satisfying of my railway career.

Above: *No 47033* The Royal Logistics Corps *looking very smart in Railfreight Distribution livery at Redmire after heading the first MOD service train along the reopened Wensleydale line on 14 February 1997. In the background is No 47213, details of which appears on page 93.*

No 47033 entered traffic at Cardiff as No D1613 in August 1964, and put in 26 years' service on the Western Region at all the main depots before being allocated to Tinsley for one month in January 1990, returning to Cardiff until November; it then went to Immingham, and eight months later, in July 1991, returned to Tinsley to join the Railfreight Distribution fleet. By April 1999 it was laid up at Bescot, and unlikely to run again.

7

Into the 90s

One outstanding feature of the class over the last few years has been the proliferation of liveries. In the 1970s, several depots had managed to break up the drab all-over blue, perhaps the most notable early example being Stratford's white roofs. (This was of course, an age-old Great Eastern tradition, that company's principal express passenger locomotives, the 'Claud Hamilton' class 4-4-0s, and their later 4-6-0 derivatives, having always had grey roofs. Later, the GE section Royal Engines perpetuated the style, both in LNER and BR days, even the 'Britannias' being so adorned.) Indeed, during HM The Queen's Silver Jubilee celebrations, Stratford decked out two of the class (Nos 47163/4) with Union Flags, one on each side, and covering the complete depth of the body-side; they also had white roofs and silver battery boxes. Stratford later went on to 'push its luck', and unofficially named No 47460 'Great Eastern', but this was, somewhat predictably, short-lived. (As mentioned in the previous chapter, No 47581 was later officially named *Great Eastern*, after BR adopted a more enlightened policy on locomotive namings.)

Some corporate break-up of the slab-sided blue came with the introduction of the large logos and numbers first seen on Class 56s, but later applied to many of the ETH-fitted Class 47s. Stratford managed on one locomotive to elongate the logo into complete body-side stripes, along with red, white and blue, at the time of the marriage of HRH The Prince of Wales to Lady Diana Spencer in 1981. Other depots played around too, principally with the introduction, usually unofficially, of depot logos, like Eastfield's West Highland Terrier, Thornaby's Kingfisher and Stratford's Cockney Sparrow.

Perhaps surprisingly, it was Railfreight that really broke the mould, with the introduction of all-over grey with red trim. This was closely followed by InterCity, Stratford Repair Shop appropriately being chosen to paint the first locomotive (No 47487) in the new livery, the work being carried out in the spring of 1985. Next came Network SouthEast, and this was a real eye-opener! Considerable behind-the-scenes planning went into the introduction of the new image for the London and South East suburban services, largely the brainchild of then newly-appointed Sector Director, Chris Green, fresh from his exploits north of the Border (where incidentally, he greatly supported the Eastfield Terrier). It was intended that at least one locomotive or train in the new livery would be running on each route on launch day, Tuesday 10 June 1986. Great secrecy surrounded the preparation of the vehicles, and No 47573 being taken out of service several weeks beforehand, and we subsequently spent many anxious hours, assisted, and very often (we felt) hampered, by the American consultants! On the eve of the launch the locomotive, resplendent in its bright new livery, went to Liverpool Street, because as part of a pre-launch celebration dinner, it was to be named *The London Standard* by that newspaper's then Editor. This was a public relations exercise, to engender the support of this paper, then as now one of BR's harshest critics. So closely guarded was the brand name and logo of the new image that neither was displayed on the locomotive, which returned to Stratford that evening so that both could be applied ready for launch day. After photography at Stratford the following morning, the locomotive went on display at Liverpool Street, before hauling the 17.30 to King's Lynn that evening. Of all the many naming ceremonies I have been involved with over the years, this was undoubtedly one of the most enjoyable, and so rewarding to be a part of the new image at its inception. Later, Stratford painted all five of its allocated NSE Class 47s in the new livery, and introduced a special 'A' examination for them, at increased frequency. This latter was due to their extensive diagramming, to the importance of the service on which they were used, and to the probable consequences of one failing on the Great Eastern during the morning and evening peaks, or on the single line between Ely and King's Lynn. So successful was this, that in the 18 months between its repainting and its subsequent transfer to Old Oak Common, No 47573 did not suffer a single traction casualty in service.

The latter half of the 1980s saw not only the sectorisation of the locomotive fleet but, particularly in the case of Railfreight, the sub-sectorisation, not only of the locomotives, but of many of the depots too. Therefore, in designing yet another new livery for this sector, to replace the then only recently introduced overall grey, a series of motifs was designed, around a corporate 'house' style. Again, Stratford was heavily involved in this, and for the launch of this new style — launching new images clearly being in vogue at that time — an exhibition was staged at Ripple Lane depot, near Dagenham, on 15 October 1987. Stratford painted examples of Classes 08, 47, 56 and 58, as well as altering a Class 37 already painted experimentally at Crewe. The choice of No 47079 to represent Class 47 caused much consternation among Western Region colleagues, as it was then painted in Great Western green, and named G. J. Churchward, having been decked out in this fashion as a part of the 1985 Great Western 150th Year celebrations. However, as Stratford was committed to painting representatives of Classes 08, 56 and 58 (all to an extremely tight timescale) before it was decided to include a Class 47 in the exhibition, the only way to accomplish this was to select a locomotive that was due for repaint anyway. Unfortunately, as far as the Western Region was concerned, the only locomotive that fell into this category was No 47079, at Stratford for one of the first 'F' examinations after introduction of the New Maintenance Policy. It really was 'Hobson's choice'!

Subsequently, other 'special' liveries have appeared, locomotives being painted to commemorate all sorts of events, like Doncaster Works open day (LNER apple green) and the 150th Anniversary of the Midland Counties Railway (LMS maroon).

During the period here under review, the locomotives have continued to be seen all over the system, despite the large inroads made into their numbers by an increased rate of scrapping. Sub-sectorisation of the fleet has seen specific members of the class restricted to particular traffic flows and, in attempts to reduce maintenance costs, the freight sector locomotives have been restricted to 75mph, as this is the maximum speed of any freight train. It has the added advantage that these locomotives can be fitted with cast iron brake blocks with a high phosphorus content; these blocks have a much longer life than the standard cast iron variety, but do have a tendency to fracture at high speeds, hence their restricted use. One of the adverse effects of sectorisation has been the confinement of a relatively small number of Class 47/4s to InterCity services. Because these are relatively small in number, all are allocated to one depot. However, their diagrams take them over most of the country, and they are accruing mileage and engine hours unequalled since the class was used on the ECML prior to the introduction of HSTs; this is having serious effects on their reliability.

The 1980s brought about a tremendous spate of locomotive namings, after a long period of apparent hostility to such events. One which my wife and I particularly enjoyed took place at Bounds Green depot on Saturday 10 March 1984, when No 47408 was named Finsbury Park, having been a long-time resident of that depot. The actual unveiling of the name was undertaken by Mrs Marjorie Page, wife of the one-time Depot Manager, the late Stan Page. Stan was at Finsbury Park from its opening in 1959, and remained there until forced to retire due to ill health in 1978; unfortunately, he enjoyed only four years of retirement. It was extremely thoughtful of the then General Manager of the Eastern Region, Frank Patterson, to invite Marjorie along, and it was a great pleasure for me to be alongside them both on the rostrum, along with my old friend John Cronin, the Depot Manager, to say a few words. Subsequently, I was successful in my request of David Rayner, Frank Patterson's successor, for the nameplates to be transferred to another Class 47, No 47654 (later 47809) when No 47408 was withdrawn a few years later, and so keep the memory lingering on a little longer — it has to be added that he did not take much persuading!

On this happy note, I end my story. I left Stratford in the spring of 1989 to take up an appointment as Area Manager (Freight) for South Wales, based in Cardiff. Whilst I continued to have limited contact with the class, to all intents and purposes my personal involvement finished, after some 28 years — indeed since they were first built, as I had helped to build some of them during my time at Crewe Works. In my subsequent appointments, with Network SouthEast and, later, the RoSCos, it has been but a passing interest.

Above: No 47213 Marchwood Military Port, *in the initial Railfreight Distribution livery, is seen on 14 February 1997 shunting the MOD tank train at Redmire on the recently reopened Wensleydale branch, which originally ran from Northallerton right through to the Settle & Carlisle line at Garsdale.*

The locomotive emerged from the Brush works in May 1965 and went to Tinsley as No D1863.

Its subsequent allocations were:

9.67	Immingham
10.69	Holbeck
12.69	Tinsley
1.70	Immingham
10.81	Gateshead
1.82	Immingham
5.83	Healey Mills
9.84	Gateshead
5.85	Tinsley
6.86	Bristol, Bath Road
10.87	Tinsley
3.98	Bescot
2.99	withdrawn
	and dumped at Healey Mills.

Liveries:
BR green (from new)
BR blue, applied between February and April 1975
Railfreight, October 1986
Railfreight Distribution, October 1989 (decals removed in February 1992, but restored, with silver cab trims added, in July 1995).

Appendix I.
Official Names

Note: the number is that carried when officially named.

Number	Name	Date Named
D1660	City of Truro	6/65
D1661	North Star	3/65
D1662	Isambard Kingdom Brunel	3/65
D1663	Sir Daniel Gooch	5/65
D1664	George Jackson Churchward	5/65
D1665	Titan	8/66
D1666	Odin	3/65
D1667	Atlas	6/66
D1668	Orion	10/65
D1669	Python	3/66
D1670	Mammoth	8/65
D1671	Thor	9/65
D1672	Colossus	8/65
D1673	Cyclops	6/66
D1674	Samson	9/65
D1675	Amazon	11/65
D1676	Vulcan	10/65
D1677	Thor	8/66
47004	Old Oak Common Traction & Rolling Stock Depot	2/94
47007	Stratford	11/86
47010	Xancidae	5/89
47016	The Toleman Group	5/87
47016	Atlas	2/94
47033	The Royal Logistics Corps	5/95
47049	GEFCO	4/96
47053	Dollands Moor International	5/94
47060	Halewood Silver Jubilee 1988	10/88
47085	Conidae	8/88
47085	Repta 1893-1993	9/93
47095	Southampton WRD — Quality Approved	4/94
47114	Freightlinerbulk	5/97
47119	Arcidae	9/88
47120	RAF Kinloss	6/85
47121	Pochard	2/94
47125	Tonnidae	9/88
47142	The Sapper	10/87
47142	Traction	12/94
47146	Loughborough Grammar School	5/95
47157	Johnson Stevens Agencies	12/95
47158	Henry Ford	7/81
47167	County of Essex	7/79
47169	Great Eastern	3/79
47170	County of Norfolk	8/79
47172	County of Hertfordshire	7/79
47180	County of Suffolk	6/79
47184	County of Cambridgeshire	5/79
47186	Catcliffe Demon	4/93
47190	Pectinidae	9/88
47193	Lucinidae	8/88
47194	Builideae	8/88
47195	Muricidae	9/88
47196	Haliotidae	10/88
47200	Herbert Austin	9/94
47206	The Morris Dancer	4/94
47207	Bulmers of Hereford	12/87
47207	Felixstowe Enterprise	4/98
47209	Herbert Austin	8/90
47210	Blue Circle Cement	1/90
47213	Marchwood Military Port	6/93
47214	Distillers MG	11/90
47218	United Transport Europe	7/90
47222	Appleby-Frodingham	6/82
47223	British Petroleum	8/90
47228	axial	9/95
47231	The Silcock Express	9/88
47233	St[r]ombidae	9/88
47236	Rover Group	10/96
47238	Bescot Yard	10/88
47241	Halewood Silver Jubilee 1988	9/95
47245	The Institute of Export	7/94
47270	Cory Brothers	8/96
47278	Vasidae	11/88
47280	Pedigree	1/86
47283	Johnnie Walker	9/88
47286	Port of Liverpool	12/93
47291	The Port of Felixstowe	3/87
47293	Transfesa	11/97
47297	Cobra Railfreight	5/95
47298	Pegasus	7/90
47301	Freightliner, Birmingham	11/95
47303	Freightliner Cleveland	3/97
47306	The Sapper	4/94
47309	The Halewood Transmission	9/90
47309	European Rail Operator of the Year	4/98
47311	Warrington Yard	6/88
47312	Parsec of Europe	7/97
47314	Transmark	12/90
47315	Templecombe	7/93
47317	Willesden Yard	7/88
47319	Norsk Hydro	3/88
47323	Rover Group Quality Assured	2/94
47324	Glossidae	9/88
47326	Saltley Depot Quality Approved	12/94
47330	Amlwch Freighter/ Tren Nwyddau Amlwch	6/90
47333	Civil Link	5/90
47334	P&O Nedlloyd	10/97
47337	Herbert Austin	4/86
47348	St Christopher's Railway Home	5/81
47350	British Petroleum	4/87
47361	Wilton Endeavour	7/83
47363	Billingham Enterprise	12/85
47365	ICI Diamond Jubilee	9/86
47366	The Instition of Civil Engineers	5/86

47616	Y Ddraig Goch/The Red Dragon	6/85
47617	University of Stirling	10/84
47618	Fair Rosamund	10/84
47620	Windsor Castle	8/85
47621	Royal County of Berkshire	6/85
47622	The Institution of Mechanical Engineers	5/87
47624	Saint Andrew	5/94
47627	City of Oxford	5/85
47630	Resounding	7/93
47631	Ressalder	9/93
47635	Jimmy Milne	4/87
47636	Restored	3/93
47636	Sir John de Graeme	4/86
47637	Springburn	6/87
47638	County of Kent	6/86
47639	Industry Year 1986	6/86
47640	University of Strathclyde	4/86
47642	Strathisla	9/86
47644	The Permanent Way Institution	6/86
47645	Robert F. Fairlie	5/86
47654	Finsbury Park	8/86
47673	InterCity Route Control York	3/94
47701	Saint Andrew	1/79
47701	Waverley	5/97
47702	Saint Cuthbert	3/79
47702	County of Suffolk	2/94
47703	Saint Mungo	3/79
47703	Lewis Carroll	3/95
47704	Dunedin	2/79
47705	Lothian	4/79
47705	Guy Fawkes	7/95
47706	Strathclyde	5/79
47707	Holyrood	5/79
47708	Waverley	6/79
47709	The Lord Provost	9/79
47710	Sir Walter Scott	10/79
47710	Lady Godiva	6/94
47710	Quasimodo (temporary)	5/96
47711	Greyfriars Bobby	4/81
47711	County of Hertfordshire	6/93
47712	Lady Diana Spencer	4/81
47712	Dick Whittington	6/95
47713	Tayside Region	5/85
47714	Grampian Region	5/85
47715	Haymarket	8/85
47716	Duke of Edinburgh's Award	7/85
47717	Tayside Region	9/88
47721	Saint Bede	6/95
47722	The Queen Mother	8/95
47725	The Railway Mission	6/95

47726	Manchester Airport Progress	11/95
47726	Progress	11/95
47727	Duke of Edinburgh's Award	10/94
47732	Restormel	7/95
47733	Eastern Star	9/95
47734	Crewe Diesel Depot	3/96
47736	Cambridge Traction & Rolling Stock Depot	3/94
47738	Bristol Barton Hill	2/94
47742	The Enterprising Scot	7/95
47743	The Bobby	3/95
47744	Saint Edwin	3/95
47744	The Cornish Experience	10/97
47745	Royal London Society for the Blind	9/93
47746	The Bobby	11/95
47747	Res Publica	6/94
47749	Atlanta College	11/95
47750	Royal Mail Cheltenham	3/96
47756	Royal Mail Tyneside	7/95
47757	Restitution	4/94
47758	Regency Rail Cruises	9/98
47760	Ribblehead Viaduct	4/99
47767	Saint Columba	6/96
47770	Reserved	6/94
47773	Reservist	6/94
47781	Isle of Iona	7/95
47783	Saint Peter	6/95
47784	Condover Hall	8/94
47785	The Statesman	7/95
47785	Fire Fly	3/97
47785	Fiona Castle	6/97
47786	Roy Castle OBE	7/94
47787	Victim Support	12/94
47788	Captain Peter Manisty RN	1/93
47789	Lindisfarne	2/95
47790	Saint David/Dewi Sant	3/95
47791	Venice Simplon Orient Express	12/94
47792	Saint Cuthbert	5/95
47793	Saint Augustine	6/96
47798	Prince William	5/95
47799	Prince Henry	5/95
47803	Women's Guild	6/89
47803	Midland Railway Trust	10/93
47807	The Lion of Vienna	4/98
47810	Porterbrook	3/96
47813	SS Great Britain	4/98
47814	Totnes Castle	5/97
47816	Bristol Bath Road	5/95
47822	Pride of Shrewsbury	5/98
47831	Bolton Wanderer	6/89
47973	Derby Evening Telegraph	9/90